NOTHING LIKE A DANE

Nothing Like a Dane

A real-life search for hygge in Denmark

KERI BLOOMFIELD

PEMBAR
PRESS

For Dad & Ida

Contents

"**Hygge** is about an atmosphere and an experience, rather than about things. It is about being with the people we love. A feeling of home. A feeling that we are safe, that we are shielded from the world and allow ourselves to let our guard down."

– **Meik Wiking**, author of *The Little Book of Hygge*

Introduction

I walked naked across the changing room pretending it was the most natural thing in the world. It wasn't, of course: in 36 years, my New Zealand birthday suit had never been seen in public. I was completely out of my depth and hadn't even made it to the swimming pool yet.

As I reached the showers, I froze like a deer in the headlights. I was aware my own headlights were on full-beam too, though I didn't look down to check. In front of me lay a sea of bums and boobs. A communal shower full of women evidently more liberated with their bodies than me, were scrubbing their underarms and groins with remarkable vigour. Meanwhile my own DNA from another land recoiled in horror. I'm the first to admit that growing up on a remote South Pacific island has left me, paradoxically, a little sheltered in my views to nudity.

My significant other – 'The Dane' as I liked to refer to him, partly because it was easier to pronounce than his Danish name – had told me I'd need a shower before swimming. An innocuous suggestion I'd dismissed until I was staring straight down an aisle of bare-skinned butts of every shape, with mine about to join them. I was every inch a stunned prude.

We have the same logic in New Zealand, of course: one should be clean before swimming. But our execution of this theory is worlds apart. Showers in New Zealand have curtains and are rarely communal. Always, there are individual changing cubicles available for those who've not yet mastered yanking off a wet swimsuit beneath an oversized towel before pulling their undies up over damp legs. Showering is also, in most cases, done in *togs* (swimsuit to the rest of the world). Groins are not heartily scrubbed in public.

Staring at my showering companions I was thankful of having a minute social circle in Denmark. The odds were in my favour that I was unlikely to run into someone I knew while starkers.

Those 20 minutes became the longest of my Danish life. To reach the showers, I first had to navigate a terrifying one-way maze in a bare-arsed state. My shoes came off first (and to be fair, that bit was quite easy) before I found a locker to hover in front of while calculating my escape through the overwhelming nakedness around me. Women were blow drying their hair au naturel while making casual chit chat. A swimming attendant circled, wearing a bright red and yellow shirt and shorts combo (grossly overdressed given the environment). She patrolled the changing rooms ensuring everyone was appropriately cleaning themselves – I watched in horror as she sent another woman back for not washing her hair. After many moments of indecision, I had no choice but to drop my pants and stuff them in my locker. Clutching my swimsuit and towel hard, I strode disrobed towards the showers.

If there was an illustration to sum up my vulnerability and awkwardness in this new land among Danes, this was it. Standing without a stitch on, 18,000km from New Zealand, in a room full of equally bare-arsed women, I knew I was different to the Danes. Even if they weren't giving my four white cheeks a second glance.

If you've lived with anyone from another culture, you'll understand. Square pegs don't fit in round holes.

When I first moved to Denmark, the differences were jarring. It was easy to make sweeping statements about another culture based on the most noticeable behaviours. Part fiction, part fact, it was something both locals and foreigners liked to play. *Locals do this... foreigners do that... locals are crazy because they do this... foreigners are crazy because they do that...* It's an easy habit to slip into. After all, bad eggs float to the surface and are the ones you notice first. They're also the ones that make the best stories.

I used to have a life in New Zealand. An ordinary life, speaking my mother tongue, English; surrounded by friends and family; and a career. A life that was easy to navigate, and one where I wasn't a foreigner.

But then a sliding doors moment happened. A split-second decision to look right instead of left one night at a crowded bar in my hometown of Wellington. That was all it took to begin my journey towards life in Denmark. A similar scenario to the one that lured Tasmanian Mary just a few years earlier from Australia to Denmark, where she became Princess Mary.

After one of the world's longest flights (17.5 hours plus another eight for good measure) I arrived in Denmark in 2016 with a four-month-old baby, two suitcases and no friends. You can liken the feeling to being placed in a tumble dryer with the lights out: you'll go around and around, occasionally hitting the wall with no idea really where you are. Geographically or mentally.

To make sense of my new life, I began sharing some of the cultural challenges. Most of these ramblings were shared in my *Bilingual Backpack Baby* blog and gave me purpose in my new life. It also led to other opportunities, including writing for the Danish newspaper, *The International*. This book is the story of what happened in between those cultural learnings.

In an attempt to not create an undue number of awkward encounters in my life, some names have been changed and my portrayal of some characters are a combination of various people that have crossed my path. I have also purposefully chosen to keep my family in the background throughout the book to ensure awkward moments around the family dinner table are minimised.

Lastly, to help you navigate any unknown Danish or New Zealand words and phrases, you can find a glossary at the back of the book.

I hope it entertains.

One, Meeting The Dane

The Pizza

I saw his pizza first.

It lured me in with its crispy crust, as all thought of my friends waiting for me to return with the next round of drinks flew out of my head.

Unable to find a seat in the popular Malthouse brewery, he'd been standing at the bar with a beer in one hand and a pizza perched in front of him. Approaching from behind, I'd done my best impersonation of a salmon swimming upstream as I tried to push my way through the crowd towards the bar in the hope of ordering another round. On either side of us, the after-work crowd was in high spirits, becoming louder and drunker by the minute.

"Are you going to eat all of that?" I asked, barely registering what he looked like as I waited for my drinks, my eyes fixed on the remaining slices of pizza that lay on a trendy longhandled wooden platter. I stared so hard I noticed the dusting of flour under the pizza that stopped it sticking. *A clear sign of hunger,* I thought.

It was a warm February night in Wellington, the kind that makes you wonder why you would want to live anywhere else in the world.

While the summer holiday season had now ended and the school year had begun the great weather still lingered. It was a perfect social storm, enticing the nearby office workers to the buzz of Courtenay Place, with its never – ending selection of bars, restaurants and clubs. It was the sort of night that doesn't happen too often, but when it does, you can almost see the magic in the air. The universe had aligned to create a warm evening with full wine glasses, laughter filling the bars, and no one in a rush to go home.

Shit, that pizza looks good. Dripping with cheese and fresh herbs, it spoke directly to the cavernous pit in my stomach that was in survival mode searching for food. Presumably, it was the reason my heart skipped a beat while I waited for Pizzaman to reply to my question.

"Help yourself," he said, shrugging his shoulders in bemused bewilderment. I couldn't quite place the accent. *German perhaps? Or was it Dutch? Interesting,* I thought, as I ate his pizza, the cheesy goodness sliding down with minimal effort to my waiting stomach. Pizzaman looked at me with a hint of justified confusion on his face.

I guess wherever he came from he wasn't used to strangers talking to him, let alone eating his food.

"Where are you from?" I asked, going in with the big question, but then not waiting for his answer (patience has never been my thing). I followed up swiftly with, "Germany? Are you from Germany?" as the alcohol fearlessly encouraged my line of questioning.

"No," came the sharp, one-word answer.

Hmmm, I thought, *Pizzaman will need a bit more warming up if this conversation is going anywhere.* Always up for a challenge, I cheekily picked up the wooden platter holding what remained of his pizza and offered him a piece.

A smile, possibly a grimace, moved over his face as he replied, "Denmark".

An image of pastries and a pint-sized mermaid statue immediately jumped into my head. "Ahhhh, Denmark. Been there, done that," I said (with the naivety of a child). "Good pastries. Not sure about the brown bread and herring thing, though. Anyway, come and meet my friends so we can swap travel stories." I pointed at my group of friends sitting on the other side of the bar. Without giving him a chance to answer, I took his pizza paddle, manoeuvring it through the crowd to the table where the rest of my group had been gathered since our arrival five hours earlier.

I'd travelled around Europe in my 20s and remembered how magical it was when a local embraced us, buying us a drink and sharing a few stories for no other reason than just because they could. These were the unscripted, magical moments of travelling. I assumed, as a solo traveller, Pizzaman would enjoy the same opportunity.

My friends graciously welcomed my catch into the group like they always did.

"Again, Keri?" Lisa chortled as she stifled a howl of amusement, referring to my reputation of connecting with strangers.

I smiled. "Just another friend we haven't met yet," I replied. The habit had started a few years earlier at the many industry networking drinks I'd had to attend. Events where you're supposed to talk like it was the 1990s with only a watch (if you wore one) to busy yourself with as you tried to break into one of the huddled groups of strangers around you. You wait for a lull in their conversation to introduce yourself, but often end up like an awkward 13-year-old at their first school disco waiting to be asked for a dance.

My goal at these events was to make it a game to talk to strangers. I'd gone slightly off script with Pizzaman, but nevertheless the intention, aside from the pizza, had been the same: connecting with people I might not otherwise have met. The wine also helped.

An ingrained part of my DNA, along with my connector personality, resulted in a horrifying combination for those who hadn't been brought up to say 'Hello' to strangers on the street.

Shuffling over, my friends made room for Pizzaman to join the table. They were big fans of *Borgen*, the popular Danish political drama television series, and eagerly listened to his travel stories in the hope of learning more about life in Denmark.

"You cycled over the Remutakas?" Lisa asked, referring to the mountain range just north of the city. "Why would you do that? You know you can take your bike on the train, right?"

"That wasn't the point," Pizzaman replied. "I wanted to experience the country, not just look at it."

Pizzaman, as we discovered, had been working in China for the last two years as an automation engineer, expatriated by a Danish pharmaceutical company to build an insulin plant. Travelling through New Zealand on his bike was his reward after completing the contract.

"I started in Christchurch and worked my way up the east coast before heading over to Kaiteriteri and then back to Picton. Some campers in Kaiteriteri recommended this place," he said, waving his hand to reference the moderately upmarket pub we were in.

Danes love their bicycles with nine out of 10 of them owning one. Only four out of 10 Danes own a car.

As the beer continued, Pizzaman became more comfortable deciphering the New Zealand accent and slang, as well as the New Zealand strangers. His stories began to flow.

Slowly, I realised I was becoming a bit more interested in Pizzaman than his pizza. But I also knew it was his last night in New Zealand before beginning the journey back to Denmark. He was booked on the painfully early sparrow's fart flight at 6am the next day. I didn't expect to set eyes on him again. This was a night to file in the *good time, not a long time* box of life experiences. So, when I said goodbye to him later that evening outside The Malthouse, with the now very late and quite drunk crowd circling around us, I wasn't planning on seeing him again. He was flying out in just a few hours, and besides I'd eaten half his pizza and was no longer hungry, which seemed all that mattered.

"Have a safe trip back to Denmark," I offered.

"Thanks," came his short and razor-sharp answer again – a style of communication that, unbeknown to me, I was about to become much more familiar with.

Late the next morning, when he should have been somewhere over the Pacific Ocean with his phone turned off, I sent Pizzaman a text message. Within seconds a reply landed back in my inbox:

It was good to meet you too. Do you want to have coffee this afternoon?

I froze. I was confused. He should have been on the plane. Back then, international flights only left Wellington early in the morning, and by 7am his plane should have departed. It didn't make sense why was he asking me for a coffee. My phone beeped again as if he'd anticipated my confusion.

I had a problem with my ticket. Wasn't allowed on the flight. Now leaving Sunday.

Shoot. So much for a pizza with no strings attached. I'd attracted a Dane.

The Clairvoyant

Five years before asking Pizzaman if I could share his dinner, I'd sat in my car on a quiet rural road outside a clairvoyant's house. Her house was less than 500m from the main state highway, but it may as well have been a world away. Sporadically placed weatherboard homes lined the road – most of them in need of a new coat of paint. Other than the overgrown gardens tumbling from one property to the next, there was little sign of life anywhere on the road.

Arriving early, I parked next to an out-of-control hydrangea bush and did my best to fill time before my 10.30am appointment. I began cleaning out my parking money container. Fluffing around, I started sorting receipts from the coins that had congregated in the console, when my mind wandered to a mantra I'd parroted to myself over the years: *my twenties are for myself.* The phrase began to repeat itself in my head.

With a university degree, six years' work experience in New Zealand and another two in London, I'd been making progress on both the career ladder and the ladder of life – without the restraints of having to compromise with any significant other in my life. It was the upside of having been single for most of my 20s.

But as I sat, aged 29, in my car outside that clairvoyant's house, I began to wonder if I'd taken a detour from achieving what I wanted most: a house, children and a soul mate.

Wouldn't hurt to get a second opinion, I thought as I walked down the narrow and uneven garden path towards a small porch.

As she opened the door, I considered whether I needed to introduce myself to a clairvoyant.

"Come in Keri. I'm Margaret," she said, more as an instruction than an introduction.

That solves that then, I thought as I smiled in acknowledgement and followed her to a nook in her living room.

We sat on opposite sides of a small card table. Margaret on an office chair – perfect for swivelling between her cassette voice recorder and the deck of cards on the table.

I was also swivel-ready thanks to the wobbly floral piano stool I'd been directed to. Surrounding us was a large family of handmade cat dolls sitting on top of the piano. And the bookcase. And the windowsill. Noticing my eyebrows were beginning to knot together in puzzlement, Margaret caught me staring.

"They're cat people. Half-cat, half-human," she explained, smiling broadly.

That at least was obvious, I thought, looking at the cat faces that had been attached to the dolls' bodies, while willing my eyebrows to stop rising. It was more the *why* I was struggling with.

Even though Margaret had come highly recommended, this was my first time and I wasn't sure what to expect. I was nervous about hearing something I didn't want to hear, and now the half-cat, half-doll family were challenging my level of comfort. It took some minutes to relax into my new environment.

I'll take their eccentricity as a sign of clairvoyant authenticity, I thought just before she began the reading.

"You've been waiting a while," she said, staring into the three cards laid in front of her that related to finding a life partner. "Hmmm. The problem is you won't just settle for anyone. Others do, but if you don't see a future with them, then you don't waste your time going any further."

Nice validation, I thought.

"But he's coming. He's moving towards you," she said, her face scrunched in concentration as she shot a look over the top of her glasses towards a particularly scary-looking cat-doll to the left of me with a boat under its paw.

"On a slow boat from China?" I dryly joked back.

Margaret's head snapped back upright as another look shot right through me. She seemed to be trying to make sense of my joke, as if I'd just made the wildest yet most accurate statement she could imagine, similar to being told in 2010 that Donald Trump would become the President of the USA.

But she said nothing. *Perhaps I'm just not as witty as I thought.*

Unbeknown to me, at the same time I was sitting on the wobbly piano stool, Pizzaman was just months away from beginning his two-year expatriation working in Asia, the one that would eventually lead him to New Zealand.

Pizzaman had been coming from China.

Two, Saying Goodbye

Moving Day

Four years after the pizza encounter in Wellington, we woke together in our empty Auckland house, which had been our home for the past three years. Waking slowly, I could feel the air mattress had again mysteriously lost half its air overnight. We were now at the delicate point where, if one of us moved, the other would hit the floor. Undeterred by the laws of physics, The Dane, formerly known as Pizzaman, jumped out of bed in one swift movement, sending me unceremoniously to the floor. My hipbone crashed into the carpet below, ensuring I was now fully awake.

"So. That's it. Let's grab some breakfast and go." His Danish efficiency shone annoyingly bright at the early hour of 6.30am as he planned our final morning before his departure from Auckland International Airport.

After packing up, selling off and boxing up our remaining possessions into storage, the air mattress was the last piece of furniture we had in the house – if you could call it furniture. As we squeezed out the remaining air and began stuffing it back in its box, I started mentally preparing for once again having to say goodbye to The

Dane at the airport. This time, it was at least with the promise I'd be following a month later to complete our move to Vikingland, the land of hygge and low hanging lamps.

"Shall we grab a coffee from up the road?" I suggested as we waited for our landlord to arrive for the final inspection.

"Sure, I'll just finish packing the car."

I willed my eyebrows not to rise at his Danish engineering optimism. The car was already crammed to capacity and unless he was offering to ride on the roof to the airport, I wasn't sure which part of it he believed still packable.

Ordering two flat whites, we sat outside the uninspired Happy Beans cafe watching traffic crawl towards Onewa Road. The narrow car lanes bulged with traffic, flanked by two underused sidewalks. I wasn't going to miss this road, with its rollercoaster of dips and rises, and the hour-long jams to travel some 3km to the motorway on ramp. The road was a soul-killer.

After living like Kiwis, it was time to try the Viking life. Insta-grammable images of bicycles with baskets, candles and canals filled my head as I warmed my hands around my coffee. "What sort of job do you think I'll be able to find?" I asked The Dane, as I wondered what life might be like in the land of pastries with no Danish.

"You'll find a job," he replied.

Any job? Or a good job? I wondered as the next question popped into my head. "What if I get sick, before my residence permit is approved?" It was probably a conversation we should have had earlier, but with the extraordinary lead-up to our move, it had been pushed down the priority list into the pile of things to sort out when we arrived.

"It's Denmark. People aren't falling down and dying in the streets. We've got a healthcare system," he replied as his phone beeped.

"It's Christina." Our landlord, who had a desire of wanting to rule the world with her feather duster.

I'll be arriving in 5 minutes.

I was impressed how important she managed to make herself sound in just six words.

"We better head back and get this over and done with," The Dane said, grabbing his half-empty takeaway cup.

Three hours later, after surviving her final Royal inspection, I hit the indicator in our rusty Toyota Camry and merged slowly on to the motorway. Our signed-off lease form from the landlord now tucked safely in the glovebox. I looked across at The Dane in the passenger seat. He was squashed between the Electrolux and a box of possibly expired cleaning products. *He's fine,* I thought. *Good practice for 22 hours in cattle class,* I convinced myself as we pulled onto the motorway.

Arriving at the airport drop-off zone, The Dane reached for the door handle and ejected from the Camry like a jack-in-the-box, spilling out of the passenger door together with a motley bag of cleaning rags. He only just avoided being swallowed by a passing tour group marching like ants behind their leader.

"I guess I'll see you in a month?" I said, trying to picture my new life in the land of pastries.

"Remember to get a copy of the storage centre's contract," he answered, his mind still ticking over the practicalities.

No fond farewells then. "Okay, but you'll email when you change at Singapore?" I asked as a parking warden in a well-worn hi-viz safety vest began eyeing us up as he sauntered in our direction.

"I'll try. See you," he said, giving me a quick kiss before being swallowed by the tour group that was now also heading towards the terminal.

Well that was that, then. Grabbing the rags that had escaped the Camry, I threw them on the passenger seat while carefully avoiding eye contact with the parking warden. He was now lurking curbside, intent on ensuring the drop-off zone was just that. Setting the GPS for Wellington, I took a deep breath and accepted the next time I'd speak to The Dane would be from the other side of the world. *Let's get on with it then,* I thought, pulling back into the traffic and following the signs south.

The Wop Wops

What is that? I wondered as a flashing orange light penetrated my eyeballs from within the depths of the dashboard. Like a streaker on a football pitch, the blink-fest pulled my attention abruptly away from the rolling countryside. I was officially driving through the *wop wops* of New Zealand – the middle of nowhere – with only a dubious collection of AM music blaring from the ancient car radio for company. The sounds filled the remaining air pockets in the car that The Dane hadn't stuffed with our possessions.

Shit, it's the oil gauge. Kilometres of rolling green hills stretched out in front of me. The dark-grey bitumen road with its dotted white markings sliced the landscape in two like an apple pie. The only change in terrain was the occasional paddock of sheep. I contemplated how long I could keep ignoring the orange blink-fest. *If I have to stop, I need to find somewhere better than here,* I concluded as I looked out the car window, praying for civilisation, or the wop wops version of it, and soon.

As if the Camry was eavesdropping on my thoughts, the orange light began blinking even more furiously. I hit the accelerator to try to get somewhere, anywhere – wherever the heck that was – and fast. I pumped the pedal, but the car gave nothing in return, until the engine cut off with a punctuating bang. I gripped the steering wheel as my internal concern found its way to my vocal cords. "Crap!" I exclaimed, as I coasted through the approaching roundabout like a spinning bottle at the mercy of an over-excited tween as my language began deteriorating faster than a drunken sailor's. I willed my way out of the roundabout while searching desperately for a patch of gravel to pull into, before a lorry found its way up my arse.

Limping and lurching in equal measures, the Camry rolled to a slow-motion halt on a postage-stamp sized patch of grass. Smoke or maybe steam (I couldn't decide) furiously expelled itself from under the bonnet, hissing at my stupidity of ignoring its earlier warning. Grabbing my handbag and water bottle, I jumped out of the car while searching in the bottom of my Tardis-like handbag for my phone. *I really should start to put my phone in the same place in my bag in future, so I can find it in an emergency.* Eventually my hand landed on the familiar leather case. I pulled it from the depths of my bag and looked at the screen.

1:30pm

It was half an hour before The Dane's plane would take off; there was still time.

He'll know what to do, I thought, scrolling through my recent calls. I swiped his number, considering that after four years together I really should add him to my speed-dial list. *It'll be handy for times like this. Must Google how to do that,* I thought while mentally adding it to my to-do list.

"Hi?" The Dane answered, confused as he processed the pre-flight interruption. With 30 minutes to take off, he would be arranging his complimentary bag of peanuts and hand sanitiser in the seat holder while researching inflight movies for the first 12-hour leg.

"The car just exploded and there's smoke," I blurted, like a hysterical girlfriend stuck in the middle of the countryside with a carload of crap.

"It did? Exploded? We're about to take off... they just told us to turn off our phones."

"Tell me what to do." I interjected.

"Well, don't open the radiator cap. Call the AA, that's why you've been paying your car membership fee for the last 20 years, isn't it?"

"But I'm in the middle of nowhere... I'm in the wop wops," I tried explaining, using the Kiwi slang in which he was now semi-fluent. In the background I could hear a flight attendant was telling him to turn off his phone.

"I've got to go. Okay? But good luck, you'll be fine." And with a short sharp click The Dane was gone.

Two hours later I was perched on a faded orange chair with black fingerprint-shaped smears, in a small waiting room. The two mechanics who had rescued me from the side of the road were giving the Camry a onceover while I awaited their verdict. Their workshop was in a small provincial town where gumboots were the footwear of choice, even in the middle of summer. A pile of *Hot Rod* and *Classic Car* magazines sat in the corner as the only form of distraction on offer. I scrolled my phone mindlessly while resisting the urge to attack my surroundings with the packet of antibacterial wipes in my handbag.

"When was it last serviced?" the older mechanic asked me as he entered from the dark workshop with his shotgun-riding apprentice in his shadow. I'd spent an awkward 30 minutes squashed between the two of them in the cab of their tow truck as they'd hauled me to my current place of salvation. I struggled to find an answer to his question. Car maintenance had never excited me.

"Not sure," I replied. "It's my boyfriend's car." I replied using the B word, which, as it did every time, made me feel like a teenager having to refer to the man with grey highlights that I lived with as my boyfriend. Marriage had never been a priority. We were in our 30s after all – most of our friends had been there done that (in some cases, twice). And the end result didn't look any different to what the man with grey highlights and I had.

"Righto. Well, the radiator is full of rust, love. We're going to try flushing it through now and after that hopefully you'll make it to Taupo."

Taupo was my midway stop. "What happens after Taupo?" I asked, trying to work out how I was supposed to make the last 400kms before reaching Mum and Dad's at the bottom of the North Island.

"If I were you, I'd hock this off in Taupo. Get rid of it and rent a car to take you the rest of the way."

The plan sounded rather rash, but for lack of any other suggestions, I nodded in agreement and accepted it as another hurdle to navigate around.

Six Months Earlier

It had been six months since the water rushed down my legs and my heart plummeted. The water had soaked the car seat, pooling on the floor, seeping deep into Sue's upholstery.

I imagined in the future we'd find a way to laugh about destroying her car, but not right then.

"Noooooo," I whispered, inaudibly, closing my eyes as I sensed the life inside me fading, and my body emptying. I had passed the halfway point of pregnancy; the week before we'd found out we were having a girl. A growing box of baby clothes and toys had been accumulating in our spare room in anticipation of her arrival.

Sue looked at me silently, before returning her eyes to the road. I suspected she was entering her own state of shock. I was normally the bossy one, the self-appointed leader taking charge when we found ourselves in a bit of a pickle. We'd travelled to more than 40 countries together and survived a couple of years living together in both London and New Zealand, navigating plenty of unscripted episodes along the way. For those previous adventures I was always the boss bitch of sticky situations, but not tonight.

"It's not quite the work trip you'd planned is it?" I said, trying to lighten the mood as she drove furiously through a red light towards Auckland's North Shore Hospital. The Dane was in Australia for work and most likely asleep, unaware of our middle-of-the-night dash to the emergency department. Sue was miraculously in town for just one night on business – the one night I needed her.

"We're nearly there," she said, ignoring my mindless dribble, her eyes focusing on the road as her hands gripped the steering wheel harder.

I zoned out, cutting myself off from the outside world, digging deep into my mental reserves as I began processing the unthinkable.

Pulling into the hospital carpark, I looked at the clock on the dashboard.

1:46am

Hauling myself out of the car, I wondered how I could avoid making a scene on entering. *Sorry, I think I need some help?* I thought, as I mentally prepared my speech for the staff at reception. *Who the hell prepares a speech for an emergency department?*

"Can you go in first and tell them I'm here?" I asked Sue, not that it made any sense for her to do that, and rightly so she declined.

Entering the waiting room, I could mercifully see only one other person. Wearing an industrial pair of overalls, and sitting on a blue vinyl chair, hypnotised with the screen of his phone, he didn't see me. My route across the room was marked by a trail of blood and fluid on the well-trodden linoleum floor, its pattern no longer distinguishable. I didn't make it to the reception desk before a nurse appeared in front of me, preventing me going any further.

"Sorry," I said to the nurse, as her face registered what was happening.

A wheelchair appeared from behind me and I sat down uncomfortably, my insides displaced. I must have been leaving a hell of a mess everywhere.

"We'll take you up to maternity," the nurse said, balancing her levels of calm and concern while swallowing the fleeting look of shock that crossed her face, before her professional adrenaline kicked in.

"I need to move my car," Sue called from behind me. "Back in two minutes."

I nodded, wishing I was somewhere else as the nurse pushed me along the corridor and into an elevator.

I wasn't a common arrival for the maternity team, their awkwardness showed, or maybe they were just tired. I wasn't the best judge of character at that moment. But I did know it was a ward full of babies with exhausted, yet elated parents at their side. I was gate-crashing their party with my first-born daughter, Ida. Finally, 12 hours later, she was born – too early to survive. But too late not to leave an invisible and unfillable hole in me for the rest of my years. It wasn't supposed to be like this.

Final Goodbyes

"Have you bought your ticket yet?" Dad asked as he sat down for our 10 o'clock *smoko*, a tobacco-sounding break that had nothing to do with cigarettes but everything to do with home baking. He refused to relinquish the builder's tradition in his earlier-than-planned retirement – something that suited my sweet tooth since arriving at Mum and Dad's a few weeks earlier.

Carrying our mugs to the table, I wondered if he'd noticed I'd taken over tea delivery duties again. Since his stroke, his legs didn't always do what he wanted. I'd made it my job to appear in the kitchen at the right time carrying the hot mugs of milky tea to where we were sitting. It saved us both the hassle of any unplanned wrestling matches with the kitchen floormat. Enveloped by the familiarity of my childhood home, I fought hard not to turn into my 14-year-old self as we sat at the Rimu (a New Zealand evergreen coniferous tree) table that has been a fixture for at least half my life. *Bit of a mindbend,* I thought, realising my shoulders had dropped half a metre since arriving with the comfort of familiar routines. Smoko happened every day, on the dot, at 10am and 3pm. Dad was in charge of putting the kettle on, warming the teapot and preparing the cups. I'd tried to sell him on the convenience of a tea-bag for each cup, but he remained unconvinced. The teapot was where the magic happened, apparently.

"No," I replied, not entirely sure myself why I hadn't booked it. "I suppose I should?" I asked rhetorically, mainly to myself, as I disappeared back into the kitchen to grab the Ginger Crunch – a classic Kiwi slice I'd made the day before.

"It might help," Dad replied as I returned, before reaching into the Tupperware container for today's serving of home baking.

Dad had become my temporary co-worker, pottering around the house as I tidied up final work commitments from my makeshift desk, a trestle table in the spare room. When we got bored, we'd escape to one of the cafés in town for a flat white and a bit of people watching. I knew he'd much rather have been having smoko on a building site with his builder mates, but in absence of that, I was a welcome consolation prize.

Dad sucked in a gulp of air as a grimace spread across his face.

"Are you okay?" I asked, noticing his grimaces were becoming more frequent.

"Must be time for my tablets," he said, reaching towards the small dispensary of medication sitting on the bench behind us. They'd been prescribed by his cardiac specialist, who had more pills than answers. When I arrived two weeks earlier, I'd raised concern that visitors might mistake the assortment of pills in the kitchen for a new dieting trend.

Hoping a distraction would help, I opened my laptop and pulled up the floor plans of the Copenhagen apartment The Dane and I were looking at buying. Forgetting the pain in his chest, Dad's eyes lit up as he entered virtual builder mode.

"Where's the laundry?" he asked scratching his head as he analysed the plans. "You'll need to put a laundry sink in the bathroom," he advised, measuring out the floor space.

"I'm not sure there's room," I replied. "Copenhagen bathrooms are really small. Some even have the shower over the toilet," I scandalously informed him.

"They do?" he replied shaking his head, unsure what to make of it. Neither did I for that matter, other than to keep praying our bathroom wouldn't be like that. "Hmmm," he murmured, settling down to analyse the rest of the drawings while finishing his cuppa. Leaving him to it, I headed back to my temporary office desk to Google airfares to Denmark.

One Past the Goalie

Standing in my parents' bathroom a couple of weeks later, I wasn't surprised by the two lines eyeballing me from the vanity. They confirmed what I instinctively already knew. I was pregnant again. *That's a bit of a curveball,* I thought. *I've already maxed-out my excess luggage and now I have a whole extra person to make room for.*

It was only six months since Ida had been stillborn. The grief was still raw, but at 38 there was no luxury of grieving before conceiving again. The two lines were much wanted, even if they were throwing a small spanner in the works.

I turned on my computer and sent The Dane a Skype message.

Congratulations. You slipped one past the goalie.

It was the middle of the night in Denmark. He wouldn't see the message until the morning, so without waiting for a reply, I turned off my computer. I'd talk to him later, when he woke up.

"Just going for my walk, Dad." I yelled as I headed outside into the fresh air for my daily loop along the river trail. Growing up here, I'd been blinded to the beauty of the park that sat just behind Mum and Dad's home. But now as I contemplated my move to Vikingland, with its pancake-flat landscape and high-density living, I was trying to make the most of the easy access to nature. I was also hoping the fresh air would help me process the changing timeline now that I had a hitchhiker on board. I hit 'Record' on my Strava app and began walking briskly. Thoughts began to flow as unpredictably as the Hutt River running alongside me, which was struggling to process last night's downpour. Losing Ida was devastating in a way that's only comprehensible if you've experienced the same. Even the most empathetic soul would struggle to know what it feels like, until it happens to them.

When I was pregnant with Ida, I kept the news quiet for a long time, preferring to get to the falsely advertised safe zone of 12 weeks before saying anything. I'd learnt the hard way that 12 weeks was a mythical safe zone. The doctors weren't able to tell me why it happened, they'd only been able to tell me that 80% of stillbirths went unexplained. Perfect in every other way, Ida was just too small to live. The Dane had had to sprint back from Australia to meet his stillborn daughter. As I moved forward, I began to look normal to the outside world again, even though nothing had changed inside me. The grief remained carved into my soul, and now just hung invisibly and heavily on my previously naïve shoulders. Denmark or not, whatever came next in our lives, this new pregnancy would be the first priority.

A few hours later after returning from my walk, I started packing up my work desk for the day. I shutdown my laptop when my phone beeped.

What Goalie?

Oh. I've done it again, I thought, realising I'd bamboozled The Dane using a random English phrase he'd yet to discover.

Deciding it was better to get straight to the point than confuse him with any more foreign sayings, I replied with the facts:

I'm pregnant.
You are?
Yes.
So when are you coming to Denmark?

And just like that we were into the practicalities.

I'll call you after dinner.

I typed back, deciding social media platforms were not the best place for big life conversations.

"Until my residence permit comes through, I can't get my registration number, which means I can't work or get access to the healthcare system, right?" I asked The Dane as I tried to get my head around Vikingland's immigration process. I'd barely paid attention to it, until now.

"I don't think so," he replied.

Reassuring, I thought. "Yeah, nah," I replied. "I'll move when I get my paperwork approved and we know for sure I'll have access to everything." I decided that New Zealand was the safest option for me and the hitchhiker. Counting out the weeks based on the supposed processing time, the permit would be coming through when I hit 15 weeks of pregnancy. *That'll be manageable, I'll wait until then before I move.*

Laughing to himself, and barely able to finish the joke, Dad sought clarification on the situation. "Hold on. You're pregnant. Due in eight months, and The Dane left the country two weeks ago?" He put his cup of tea down and counted the months on his well-worn builder's fingers, all ten of them, which he'd told me was a sign of a good builder.

"Oh, wait until the neighbours figure this one out," he laughed reaching for another cheese scone, today's smoko treat.

I had to agree it was a tight timeline, the kind a conspiracy theorist would have enjoyed dissecting. "Well, we're heading into winter, bulky clothes and puffer jackets will hide my stomach for a while. They won't even know before I leave."

"You can try and make it on the plane before someone notices," Dad replied still laughing. Excitement shone in his eyes as he likely was beginning to plan his first round of pull-my-finger jokes for his grandchild. "But good luck!" he hooted.

Are You Coming?

Have you heard yet?

The Dane's message popped up on my phone, interrupting me as I raided Mum's wardrobe for a pair of shoes to fit my swollen feet. Pregnancy was inflating them with all the gusto of helium, increasing their girth daily. It was 20 weeks since The Dane had left New Zealand and 21 weeks since I shipped my winter wardrobe to Denmark – the small suitcase of summer clothes I had with me became officially as useless as a white crayon. My wardrobe was too small and too summery. Pregnant, barefoot and living with my parents, I felt like a teenager trapped in a 38-year-old's body.

Nothing...

I quickly typed while using my other hand to search in the far corner of the poorly lit wardrobe for the final matching black flat. The Danish immigration department had now said it could take up to six months to process my permit.

But the doctor said I shouldn't travel after 20 weeks, because of my history. She said I was high risk.

Thankful for the extra monitoring, I'd been visiting the high-risk maternity clinic every other week. They didn't have the best-looking spot in the hospital: shoved into a spare space off the main lobby with no natural daylight; an eclectic mix of 1980s sofas in the waiting room that threatened to swallow the next heavily pregnant woman who dared to sit on them.

So, are you still coming?

I should probably call him, I thought as I gave up on the hunt for the other shoe. I hoped the box full of clothes that had now arrived in his small Copenhagen apartment was enough of a sign I was coming, but I could see how he might be beginning to doubt my intentions. Kicking off the one shoe I'd been able to find, I hauled myself on to the bed to call him – by the sounds of efficient slurping, he was eating his breakfast.

"I'm not comfortable coming until I get my residence permit approved," I said.

"So you'll move after you have the baby then?"

"I guess that's how it'll work," I answered, not really having thought about that part of the situation. "But is that the right thing to do? What do you think?"

"Life's not that exciting here by myself. But I get it. We can do it that way."

My shoulders dropped half a metre as he agreed with my logic. I really couldn't imagine being anywhere else right now until the paperwork was sorted.

Every resident of Denmark is assigned a civil registration number (known more commonly in Danish as a CPR
number). You need it to open a bank account, access your
health insurance, borrow books from the library, pay tax,
receive a salary, etc. It is a combination of your birthdate
plus four unique numbers. Without a CPR number, life is
difficult.

The Last Smoko

"What's that smell?" Dad yelled, gagging in a horrified tone from the car boot where he was loading our jackets. Making the most of his release from hospital the day before, we were about to head uptown to the local café for our afternoon smoko. Hospital admissions were now a regular fixture as his stomach and chest pains became more persistent. The doctors were playing with his daily cocktail of tablets, but they only ever gave partial relief, with no one seeming to know which way the day would go.

Sitting in the car I couldn't smell anything out of the ordinary. I took another deep sniff to see what I was missing. *Was there a dash of wet carpet in the air?* I unbuckled my seatbelt and joined Dad behind the car, to see what the fuss was about.

"Oh my God, what is that?" I retched, grabbing my mouth and nose in a bid to stave off the offensive stench.

"What have you had in here? A dead cat?" he asked while pulling up the carpet in the boot to check for signs of life, or death.

"Nothing," I said, as I tried to remember the last time I'd borrowed Jeff. Jeff was the name we'd given to the small automatic runabout that now appeared to be harbouring a carcass.

"What's that?" he asked, pointing to a brown mass wrapped in plastic that had fallen into the emergency tool nook. Holding my nose, I took a closer look as I tried to read the partially visible label.

Beef Roast...Silverstream New World. Best Before 15 October.

"Oh. It's the roast I bought on special!" I exclaimed, as if the fact it was on sale went some way towards explaining why it was still sitting there. *Was that two weeks ago?* The smell was so putrid it might well have been. Scooping it up in an old paint bucket I grabbed from the garage, I tossed the package into the wheelie bin and quickly slammed the lid.

"Chicken tonight then?" he asked, as we reversed out of the driveway with the windows fully down.

Ten minutes later, we sat down at a corner table of a high street café. Passing his coffee to him, we shared an unreasonably monster-sized piece of brownie while he looked around the café.

"I came here once when your mum was in hospital and they talked to me like they had an apple up their bum," Dad said.

Somehow I managed to stop the coffee in my mouth from erupting noisily from my nostrils.

"Why didn't you say before? We should have gone somewhere else if they're a bunch of muppets," I offered, offended on Dad's behalf while also deciding I'd never come back here again.

"I think they've got new owners now. But see there?" Dad pointed at a group of tradesmen clutching their coffees in takeaway cups hovering on the pavement outside. "That was never a thing in my day. They weren't used to builders coming in by themselves and asking for a coffee 20 years ago. Ruined the look of the place I suppose. But they must have worked out it's good money." Dad paused as he searched for a sugar pourer on the table next to us. "It's been good having you at home."

"For the coffees and cakes?" I quipped, trying to lighten the moment while desperately imprinting every part of this conversation in my memory. Dad's health was getting worse and after moving to Denmark, I wasn't sure how many more chances I'd have like this. Just him and me having a coffee, in a café run by people with apples up their bums.

"For the company. It's been good to have someone else in the house while Mum's at work." He always referred to Mum as Mum, and never by her first name when talking to me, even at 38. "And to get to meet baby too, of course," he added nodding at my stomach which, giant brownie aside, was now well past the point of being concealed by a puffer jacket. It protruded to such a degree I was now unsure what my feet looked like.

For the last few months, our days had been a comfortable pattern of sharing smokos together at precisely 10am – the only exceptions being if Dad had been admitted to hospital. We each had a hospital bag packed at the ready 24/7.

Waddling back from the bathroom, I saw Dad had struck up a conversation with an old workmate, another old-school builder. I stood to the side, flipping through some outdated and coffee-stained magazines to give them some more time enjoying sharing a yarn. As much as Dad enjoyed our chats, I knew he missed connecting with his building mates from his 45-year career. It was a network that, bar a couple, had pretty much disappeared when his health turned to custard. Meanwhile, I happily embraced our father-daughter smokos.

Tutti Flutey

Two months later, a ripper of a fart tore through the hall. Wisely, the culprit, the smallest person in the room, remained hidden in her pram as the explosion reverberated throughout the congregation. It broke the one-minute of silence.

If he'd been there, Dad would have delighted at the most unfortunate-yet-remarkable timing possible for the eruption of laughter now trickling through the gathering. *Has he already worked out a way to tell his pull-my-finger Dad joke from the other side?* I marvelled. He'd been so excited about his granddaughter's arrival. The precious six weeks they'd spent together made her the obvious choice of partner for this practical joke. As a new-born baby, she had a licence to fart and people would still say 'how cute'. *Thank God he didn't pull my finger,* I thought as I pondered the universe and its powers.

Gripping my notes in my hands – single-sided print, 20 point font – I stared at the coffin within arm's reach of me. Dad's coffin.

At least I think it was. We'd been asked if we wished to view him, and a part of me wanted to double-check they'd put him in the right box, because it's a lot of trust to put in a service provider you've not met before, isn't it? In the end my brother and I had declined, but that fart was a sign, to me at least, that Dad was definitely in the coffin in front of me.

I wiped my clammy hands on my trousers which thankfully, post-pregnancy, just fitted. It hadn't been the ideal writing environment to summarise my dad's life, between nappy changes and feeds, but I just needed to deliver it now without dissolving into pieces. The fart a welcome distraction as I gripped my speech notes.

Six weeks after the fart perpetrator was born, Dad's health had plummeted. Writhing in pain on his bed at home, he'd refused to let us call the ambulance, instead he pushed his face into his pillow to muffle his groans. The man who rarely argued or raised his voice was now fighting not only his body, but also his family as we asked him if we could call an ambulance.

We'd tried hard to respect his wishes, calling instead the hospice doctor who'd made a home visit the week earlier. He was old school, and arrived dressed in smart khaki trousers, a pale blue shirt and a sensible diagonal patterned tie from the 1980s. He carried an impeccably well-conditioned brown leather doctor's bag, one I imagined he'd received as a graduation present decades earlier and had been using ever since. In comparison, I felt woefully underdressed in my baby vomit-stained maternity top and jeans, the same ones I'd been wearing all week. Thankfully, Dad had raised the bar on our side, wearing his good pair of jeans and work shirt for the occasion.

The doctor hadn't brought any magic solutions. But he did emit care and professionalism with his thoughtful and deliberate words, as he gave us his full attention at that moment, which was at least something.

As the waves of Dad's intolerable pain got stronger, the day slipped towards late afternoon and we eventually did call that ambulance. Paramedics quickly determined he needed to be taken to hospital. I supported Dad under his arms as we followed the ambulance officers down the hallway. Every time he went to hospital he'd always wanted to walk into the ambulance. He hated it when they suggested using the stretcher, because that was for 'sick' people.

We spent the next five days squashed into his hospital room. A new-born baby, me, Mum and my brother Daryl – we slept in chairs and a poorly-designed fold-out bed that had a metal pole protruding halfway through it. The fart perpetrator had fared better, with a Perspex crib on loan from the maternity ward, where she'd entered the world six weeks ago. We ate microwave meals and, like zombies, stared into space a lot.

The pain medication was so high that Dad was no longer able to communicate with us. We sat watching for his last breath. It took five days. He waited for his birthday on the 27th of December. When it happened, and for the second time in two years, I felt the air leave me as my body filled with grief. There were to be no more smokos now.

As a nurse wheeled him out to the mortuary, I whispered 'tutti flutey.' Dad and I had created this made-up phrase years ago. One that only the two of us used, never recognising it as something special, until now.

Three, Pastry Therapy

Scandi Sameville

"Fark a duck. They're all the same." The words flew unsupervised from my mouth as the taxi ground to a halt outside our new home in a street I'd yet to master pronouncing.

"What's the same?" The Dane asked, distracted as he searched for his phone to pay the driver.

How does that even work? I wondered, making a note to investigate this new payment method later.

"Them," I said, waving at the blatantly obvious. "The apartments." I pressed my nose against the taxi window, squinting to get a better view of Scandi Sameville. After 22 hours in a plane with our now four-month-old, and a night in a soulless Dubai hotel that had more gold wallpaper than anyone ever needed in their life, I was struggling to understand our new reality. The Dane, to his credit seemed to be outwardly doing remarkably well, having only just met his daughter a few days earlier. Rubbing my jet-lagged eyes, I caught the first glimpse of our new Danish apartment, feeling like I was an observer in someone else's life.

Lining both sides of the street, identical brick buildings were separated by a one-way road. Like a visual assault on my senses, the repetitive monochrome pattern confirmed that rolling countryside of hills, bush, streams and sheep would no longer be a part of my new life in Vikingland. In their place stood slabs of concrete, bricks, bicycle racks and blandness. The closest thing to nature was a row of roughly pruned trees lining the entire street, waiting for their next leaf instalment to arrive in a few weeks' time. Quickly doing the math, I figured there must have been at least 500 people living in this 500m street, one for every metre. *They'd be having kittens in Kiwiland if they tried implementing this housing model concept,* I thought.

Despite Scandi Sameville's high-density housing and threats of the masses, the neighbourhood was devoid of life. Looking along the street, the only movement on offer was a startled cat scuttling under a parked car. *Well, this is going to be different,* I thought as I tried not to take the cat antics personally.

Taking a deep breath, I grabbed my oversized handbag, spewing with baby-related paraphernalia most of which I didn't end up using during our 36-hour journey across the world. Then with the efficiency of a Nepalese Sherpa I strapped the hitchhiker – now informally named Bilingual Backpack Baby (BBB) – into my BabyBjörn backpack carrier. I kicked open the taxi door with my remaining free limb like a mama kangaroo protecting her young. A Viking on a bike seemed to greet me as the door swung open – zooming past in a blur. The joy of sighting life on our new street was short lived as the Viking began hollering and lifting his arm in a manner I was fairly sure wasn't how he'd greet his mother.

"*Hvad laver du!*" yelled the Viking on the bike.

"Huh?" I offered by way of a reply, oblivious to what we were talking about although suspecting I'd just received a Copenhagen welcome of a different sort. I shuffled my sorry arse over to the sidewalk feeling as dizzy as a pony on a merry-go-round. The cool wind slapped my face as I waited for The Dane to collect our meagre life possessions

– three suitcases, one car seat and a pram – to start our new life in the land of the Vikings. There was no shipping container to follow.

Overhead, the sky was pressing down on me, suffocating my senses like a heavy blanket of enforced hygge. The cold air found its way to **BBB** as she whimpered at the new landscape.

"Let's get upstairs," The Dane said, joining us on the sidewalk, somehow bringing order to our awkwardly-sized possessions as he moved them in the direction of our stairwell.

Huddling in the tiny doorway, The Dane jiggled the key in the lock as we waited anxiously for him to grant us access to our new life. Attempting to escape the wind from whistling through my inappropriate cotton top, I buried my face next to the letterboxes of our soon-to-be neighbours, surprised to see my own name staring at me. Taking a step back, I realised all the neighbours' names were detailed boldly in black letters on each letterbox.

Apartment addresses in Denmark are a combination of letters and numbers that relate to where your apartment is physically situated. Your address indicates what floor your apartment is located on and if you are on the left, right (and sometimes middle) of the stairs. As an example, 1TV indicates you are on the first floor to the left (TV = *til venstre*). 1TH indicates your apartment is on the first floor to the right (TH = *til højre*) and 1MF means the apartment is on the first floor in the middle (MF = *midt for*). Deciding which doorbell to ring is an unexpected minefield if people don't give their full address. Especially if you don't know the first and last name of who you are visiting (which can happen more often than you think).

Surveying the personalised letterboxes, that I presumed were a helpful initiative to avoid the awkwardness of living next to someone but never knowing their name, I considered how I felt about my name plastered outside for the world to see. *It'd be more helpful, if I knew how to pronounce their names,* I contemplated.

"Why are our names here?" I asked The Dane, pointing at the selection of doorbells and letterboxes.

Staring at me, a look of confusion spread over his face before he replied slowly, "Because we live here."

"But everyone can see them. What about privacy?"

"For a doorbell?"

"Yeee-ah." My voice faded as I started to question who the odd one was in our relationship. "For a doorbell..."

"What's wrong with people seeing our names?" he said, unlocking the door and beginning to haul our luggage up the stairs towards our new home. My privacy concerns were put on pause as we climbed two more flights of stairs where I found another door with our names displayed boldly on it. *What the feck is this?* I murmured in confusion to myself.

"On this door too?" I asked, staring at the new phenomenon of a roll call on the door of each apartment. "You'd never get away with this in New Zealand." I marvelled in bemusement.

"Every house has it," The Dane replied. "If your name's not there, then you won't get your mail," he stated before pushing open the door into our new home. A wave of woeful unpreparedness for my new life in Denmark washed over me as he did.

A Table, Two Chairs and a Bed

"Here we are. Home," declared The Dane, swinging back the apartment door to reveal a construction zone of tools, paint and a raw, grey concrete slab for a floor. As the dust cloud settled I saw a hi-viz vest – or as The Dane called it, a 'high wiz west' – hanging over a paint-splattered wooden ladder on the other side of the room.

I'd never felt so ripped off. The endless hygge hype and my own expectations of beautiful Scandinavian design being epidemic in the country were, it seemed, fake news, and well off the mark. *Possibly a bit bloody early to be referring to this building zone as a home,* I thought looking around the work site. *Full credit for being an optimist though.*

I tried to rein in my gaping mouth and swallow the shock before it triggered the sea of tears that I could feel rising from deep within. The 24-hour flight from New Zealand with its 12-hour stay in a transit hotel officially had me at my weakest.

Taking a deep breath, a chestful of dust entered my lungs and immediately began trying to exit again. Spluttering, I stammered, "Where's the floor?" My feet refused to move any further inside the apartment as I began coughing uncontrollably. "And why is there a toilet in the kitchen?" I'd been warned that Copenhagen bathrooms were suffocatingly pint-sized, but no one had mentioned having a loo in the kitchen.

"That toilet's going, once the plumbing is sorted," he replied.

For the moment, **BBB** seemed blissfully unaware of our home renovation fate. Squeezing her chubby thighs, I willed her to wake up and give me a sign of what she thought of it all. The thigh-squeezing only encouraged her to burrow further into my chest as if it was a giant sandpit. During her incubation period on the other side of the world, The Dane had been tasked with finding our Danish home in Copenhagen, the capital of cool. He was searching for the impossible in a notoriously difficult housing market. Something I hadn't given him much sympathy for at the time, my thoughts instead distracted with my task of incubating a human being.

After finding the apartment, the job then became physical with the complete gutting and renovating of our soon-to-be-home, making better use of the space. The Dane had already spent most of the previous three months knocking down walls, building new ones, ripping up floors and creating daily dust storms that were possibly visible from space, in an attempt to get the apartment ready before we arrived.

Unwilling to concede The Dane had had the hardest job, I chose to avoid any discussion regarding whether producing a human or procuring an apartment in the capital city of Denmark had been the toughest task. From where I was standing in the dust zone of home improvements, the answer was obvious. *It was me. I think.*

To be fair, The Dane had found a rare double apartment that was just a 24-minute commute on bike, traffic lights willing, from the city centre. Before we arrived, he'd told me it was in a modern building of 1930s vintage, giving me hope we'd also avoid the fate of sharing an outdoor communal bathroom – something else I'd been told still existed in the very old apartments. Aside from the thin layer of dust now residing in my chest, I reminded myself we were winning – we weren't homeless – and bravely took a big step over the collection of paint buckets, timber and tools into the apartment. Following The Dane around the building site, the short-term prognosis didn't get much better. *Well at least we've got our own bathroom,* I thought as he flicked the strangely – placed bathroom light switch in the hallway, before opening the door. The action revealed a small tiled room with nothing but a miniature sink inside. *So much for a laundry sink, Dad,* I mused as those hopes evaporated out the bathroom ventilation system. Suppressing my shock, I breathed in before asking where the toilet and shower were.

"We will have our own shower, won't we?" I asked as a flash of panic entered my head.

"Not yet, but I'll install it tomorrow," he replied.

Tomorrow? I just travelled 18,000kms, I thought, holding back whatever was rising inside me as I contemplated what a jet lagged woman might look like throwing a tantrum.

"It's a bit small compared to our place in New Zealand, don't you think?" I asked.

"The average size of a Copenhagen apartment is 50m². We've got 112," he replied educating me on the new normal. Even without a working bathroom, The Dane's 112m² apartment find was at the lucky end of the apartment scale in Copenhagen.

Although sensing I wasn't quite hitting the mark when it came to being a grateful girlfriend, I still needed more clarification.

"With just one bedroom?" I queried. "Where do the kids sleep in a standard Copenhagen apartment then?"

"In the same room."

"And if they have more than one child?"

"In the same room."

I momentarily lost control of my face again as my eyebrows began knitting themselves together. *How does that even work?*

Due to the absence of any sophisticated minimalistic Scandinavian interiors, and even with our supposedly fortunate apartment status, I began wondering whether there'd been an error and I'd signed up for a different type of Danish destiny. The destiny that had been sold to me on Pinterest and Instagram was quite different. It had white walls, low hanging lamps, sheepskin throws and a simplistic arrangement of designer furniture in natural hues. Looking around the apartment I noted our assets: A small wooden kitchen table, four creaky wooden chairs, one bed, a wooden rocking chair and a baby bed from IKEA.

The Dane's interpretation of minimalism coolness seemed to be taking it a bit far. I replaced my hopes of casually coordinated throws, cushions, candles and sheepskins, with a more modest wish of a floor and a sofa. *On the positive side, I do have a stylish and sleek designer thermal coffee pot,* I told myself as I clutched at straws, *even if it is a tad dusty and designed by a German.* I wondered whether the addition of some tea lights on the windowsills would help create the famously hyped Danish concept of hygge.

Loosely translated, hygge – pronounced *hoo-gah* – is a sense of comfort, togetherness and well-being. It is not simply wearing socks and drinking coffee in front of a fireplace (even if global marketers want you to believe that). Meik Wiking, author of *The Little Book of Hygge* describes hygge as 'an atmosphere and an experience'.

Trying to find a positive to our displaced DIY state, I began plotting an emergency trip to IKEA. Mentally clapping my hands together in excitement as I imagined exploring the Scandinavian utopia that was yet to reach New Zealand, and still retained a mythical wonderment status for me.

Pay, Pack and Get the Hell out

A month later, some of the initial shock of my new life began dissolving as the apartment's 'high-wiz west' status began to morph into something more liveable. Inhaling, my lungs now filled with hope and dust in equal measure, as the oddly placed bonus toilet was removed and we became the proud new owners of both a shower and a floor.

Looking across at The Dane, his head submerged in a kitchen cabinet, serious progress also seemed to be happening in the cooking department.

"Do you want a coffee?" I yelled at him in an attempt to be heard over his electric drill as he assembled the IKEA flatpack kitchen, something he was thankfully very good at. As well as building the kitchen, he also knew how to cook in it. It was a bit like winning the boyfriend lottery, on that front.

"Yes."

The short and sharp reply rattled my delicate buttercup native-English ears that still yearned to hear 'please' when he fired replies in my direction. I'd ignored this communication glitch at the start of our relationship, but after a few awkward encounters I eventually queried it.

"The word 'please' doesn't exist in the Danish language," he'd informed me.

At the time I thought he was joking and only after a quick Google did I fully understand what my fate would be living with a Dane. It was true, the word 'please' didn't exist in Danish. I was staring down the barrel of a lifetime without the word 'please'.

"Yes, to a coffee," he confirmed, still without the English pleasantries my brain was yearning for.

"For feck's sake," I mumbled opening the fridge as my please-less future flashed before my eyes.

"What?" The Dane called out.

"There's no milk," I artfully replied while avoiding, I hoped, the need to explain my passive aggressiveness. "I'll take BBB and get some from the supermarket."

The word *please* doesn't exist in Danish. It is instead implied with the word structure of the sentence and tone, if you're lucky. Prepare yourself accordingly when deciding to live with a Dane. For example, *'vent venligst på din tur'* means 'please wait your turn' and implies the word please by using 'venligst'. However, venligst does not on its own, mean 'please'.

Approximately 32 minutes later, after collecting everything I thought I might need for a brief outing with a baby, I carried our pram downstairs for the three-minute walk to the supermarket. With each of the 26 steps I lifted the pram down, I cursed Vikingland's lack of single-level housing. I wondered if I'd ever drop my Kiwi reluctance of leaving our pram unattended at the bottom of the stairwell. *Someone was bound to steal it, weren't they?*

Walking through the streets of Scandi Sameville, I gave myself a short pep talk: *Milk, baking margarine and* ristede løg. *I can do it.* I repeated the mantra, together with the short shopping list The Dane had thrown at me as we'd left the house. I hoped it would overcome the feelings of vulnerability I experienced at the thought of entering the supermarket solo. Feelings that were slowly turning me into a mute introvert. Defending this pathetic state, I'd tried explaining to my Danish half that it was a defence mechanism, like a tortoise's shell. Protection from being outed as the foreign pure-breed monolingual that I was. A label I'd given myself after watching the continual hullabaloo on immigration in Denmark over the last few weeks in the news. It seemed a controversial affair and

I was taking it personally as story after story rolled out that pitched Danes against foreigners reminding me, I was no longer batting for the home team. From the ongoing tightening of immigration rules, the limiting of immigrant numbers, the continual changing of immigration rules, to the repetitive reminders that foreigners must do things the Danish way. It had left me wondering if the whole nation hated everything on two legs that wasn't made in Denmark and if I was even welcome here. Acting dumb somehow eased this perplexing and tiring state as I tried to make sense of the new political climate surrounding me.

"Let's do it BBB," I said through gritted teeth, pushing her defiantly up the ramp into the supermarket, carefully avoiding eye contact with anyone as we scuttled in. Balancing the shopping basket on top of the pram, I hesitantly entered the narrow one-way shopping labyrinth in search of the milk fridge.

So far, I'd managed to avoid shopping alone. Instead, I followed The Dane around the aisles like an annoying yapping dog pushing the pram, pleading to go to a real supermarket next time, one with variety.

I've got this. Milk and baking margarine and ristede løg, I rehashed to myself peering into the foreign fridge in front of me. *I can do it.*

"What the hell is A38?" I asked BBB, picking up a carton that looked like it could be milk. "Sounds like something from the periodic table." Continuing to scan the fridge, I became overwhelmed with the foreign cartons in front of me.

Minimælk, Kærnemælk, Tykmælk, Skyr, A38.

They can't all be milk, I told myself as the raging internal debate continued over what one to choose.

A fraudulent-sounding cough burst forth from behind me, interrupting my milk deliberations. Turning around, two women, one with a dog in a basket, stood behind me. Clearing her throat,

Coughing Copenhagen Lady tilted her head while moving her eyes to the fridge behind me.

Had they been there long? I wondered, mystified as I realised this group of strangers were impersonating my mute introvert status. They were determined to get past me while avoiding any sort of eye contact or communication.

"Sorry," I said, outing myself as a foreigner as I stepped aside so they could dance awkwardly around me to the fridge.

Silently, they all reached for various cartons from the bottom shelf before turning on their heels and disappearing deeper into the maze of narrow aisles.

Taking their lead, I left the A38 dairy mystery in the fridge, and instead grabbed one of the cartons from the bottom shelf and hoped for the best. Scrambling in my pockets I pulled out the shopping list.

Milk, baking margarine and ristede løg.

Searching for the final two items, I completed an unsuccessful loop of the supermarket before passing a disproportionally large display of napkins and candles. *No room for margarine in the tiny super-market, but enough for coloured napkins and matching candles,* I questioned, as I briefly pondered a Viking's hierarchy of needs. Arriving back at the fridge of mysterious cartons, the closest relative to margarine on offer was a tub of Lurpak. Deciding it would have to suffice as baking margarine, I grabbed two. Making one last sweep in search of the ristede thingy. *Maybe it was rice?* I started to feel like Alice in Wonderland, overgrown and awkward in the impossibly tiny aisles around which I kept spiralling. Rounding the last corner, my basket became lodged between the pram and a row of tinned mackerel, halting traffic immediately as cans began to tumble down the aisle.

Cough.

Smiling weakly I turned around to see Coughing Copenhagen Lady had returned. I attempted to dislodge the shopping basket, now wedged under the mackerel shelf, while she waited with the patience of a hungry toddler.

Cough.

Discovering it only took two coughs for her to get on my wick, I wondered why she didn't just open her mouth and talk. *Maybe she has a phobia of talking to strangers?* Looking past her, my eyes fell on a display of Strepsils locked up like hard drugs next to the cigarettes and paracetamol behind the cashier. With the poise of a ballerina walking on a tightrope and the subtlety of an ox, I copied her earlier moves, and tilted my head towards the cabinet.

Giving the basket a desperate yank, it finally hurtled free together with the remaining contents on the shelf. Hurriedly pushing them back, the Coughing Copenhagen Lady scuttled past me, like an incredulous ghost set on haunting me. Restacking tins of mackerel as surreptitiously as possible, I noticed bags of rice on the shelf above. The Danish word *ris* caught my eye. Throwing one in the basket, I hoped it was close enough to whatever *ristede løg* was.

The Great Divider

I hated the dance at the checkout even more than acting like a deaf mute.

Standing in the checkout line, finally free of the fake cougher, I repeated my second survival mantra – *pay, pack and get the hell out* – as I became increasingly anxious with the impending supermarket sprint ahead of me. It was the pressure zone that had no mercy. It was where I had to somehow pay and pack for my groceries before the next customer ran me over in their quest to pack theirs. My Danish half was of course a natural at this and normally took control here as well.

Behind me, the checkout queue was growing with a range of coughing and cycling helmet-wearing Vikings all preparing for the same battle. They were blessed with the unfair advantage that they'd been training for this since birth. *How could I ever compete?* I was woefully unprepared for this contest.

Throwing the groceries onto the moving conveyor belt with one hand, I used the other to rock BBB's pram. Judging by her whimpers she, along with me, had had enough of this shopping excursion. We were both now in need of soothing.

Behind me, a helmet-wearing Viking slammed a plastic divider on the conveyor belt behind my groceries, expelling a definite breath of disapproval in my direction as he did so. *They really take the divider thing seriously here,* I thought, as I braced for the cashier to begin scanning my groceries before swiping them to the left or right, in a Tinder kind of way to my allocated side of the packing zone. There was only room for two customers in the packing zone, which made it important to finish what I needed to do fast, before the cashier began serving a third customer. If not, the whole thing would turn to custard. The fast-moving traffic in Copenhagen supermarkets made it a high-pressure socially awkward situation, especially for foreign mutes like me.

Ignoring the Viking behind me, I desperately searched for my card to get one step ahead and pay quickly. *It should be somewhere in here,* I thought as I searched in my bottomless handbag. *I never did fix this storage problem after the car breakdown in New Zealand.* Meanwhile, my groceries began whizzing past me like a bullet train. The checkout operator seemed to be training for the Perishable Goods Scanning Olympics.

"*O-da ohh elf years,*" the Olympian in training Cashier shouted Danishly in my direction requesting payment – at least that's what it sounded like to me.

"Tak," I replied with the only Danish word I'd so far mastered to offer my thanks. The word was proving useful in a variety of situations, even it wasn't always the right one. Tapping my card on the payment terminal, I tried to get to the packing zone before Viking in a Helmet's groceries barrelled in. Failing, I threw the lot into BBB's pram, the rice thankfully landing on Pop, the teddy bears', head and not hers. I scampered out of the shop as the Olympian operator continued showing no mercy with the next consignment of goods being flung down the conveyor belt.

The Cycling Embassy of Denmark (yes there really is one) advise that 32% of supermarket and street level shop purchases in Denmark are bought by people on bikes.

Emerging into the cool spring air, I felt the undeniable need for a therapeutic pastry. Something I'd unashamedly eaten a lot of since arriving.

"Let's go the long way home," I said to BBB. "Time to up our Danish pastry ratio."

Pastry Therapy

Visiting bakeries, drinking coffee and stuffing pastries in my mouth was proving an effective survival technique as I inched my way forward in Vikingland. Sanity pastry breaks had become a reason to leave the house and possibly also the reason my clothes had become a tad more fitting around my hips. Something I wasn't ready to publicly acknowledge yet.

Danishes are not Danishes in Denmark. They're called
Wienerbrød, a name given by the Austrian bakers from Vienna
(spelt 'Wien' in Danish), who first introduced them to Denmark.
That's right, Danish Pastries are really Austrian pastries.

Scandi Sameville was decorated with an eclectic mix of essential Viking shops found in most Copenhagen neighbourhoods: laundromat, a florist, a podiatrist and a tattoo shop. Like a steroid injected bee en route to its hive, we headed to what I considered the most crucial shop in the neighbourhood – the bakery. Entering with a pram was a trick though, with five high steps between us and the therapeutic pastries. Awkwardly, I thrust my arms around the pram and hauled it through the shop doors. Readjusting once I reached the top of the stairs, I spied a Viking mother parking her pram outside, leaving her baby in it, before coming into the shop. *Wild*, I thought.

Babies in Denmark typically take their naps outside in their
prams. Only when it gets colder than -10ᶜ will they come
inside to nap. This results in prams being left outside shops,
cafés and even movie theatres with sleeping babies while
parents are inside. A baby monitor tucked inside the pram
alerts the parents if they're needed.
Aside from the advantage of avoiding stairs, fresh air is
lauded as the major benefit for this habit with others saying
that the baby just sleeps better.

Hovering over the electronic ticket dispenser for my number in the queue, I tried to remember whether it was the top or bottom button I should be pushing. *One was only for pre-orders,* I thought, struggling to remember.

"Which button do you think?" I asked **BBB** in the faint hope she might guide me, but nothing, not even a burp.

Unwilling to chance anything, I hit both buttons taking the two numbers they spat out while beginning to eye up the pastry porn behind the glass counter. There were still many exotic creations to work my way through.

"*Niogtyve!*" called the blue apron-wearing bakery assistant, her hair escaping across her face from her matching hat. Looking at the screen behind her, a bright red 29 flashed at me. My number. Smiling, hopefully not too deliriously, I pointed at the biggest chocolate pastry on offer, the *direktør* something, with its golden airy pastry spiralling into a snail shell shape with a cup of dark chocolate icing poured over the top.

Hauling **BBB** back down the stairs, we headed home along the brick apartment-lined street, pushing the pram just slow enough for me to savour the sanity pastry in solitude.

Wiping any tell-tale flakes of pastry from my cheeks before entering the apartment, I dropped the milk, butter and rice on the table, the only clear surface currently available in the kitchen.

"What's that?" The Dane asked looking over at my supermarket haul.

"Milk, margarine and *ristede løg,* I hope," I said, murdering the infamous Danish letter ø – the o with a slash through it. It was a letter never encountered before moving to Denmark and knotted my vocal cords faster than a sailor tying up his boat in a storm. The Dane's face remained impassive as he questioned the foreign items on the table.

"What?" I asked searching for feedback.

"It's rice."

"I know."

"Ristede løg isn't rice. It's fried onion, the crunchy things for toppings on bread? And that's not baking margarine. It's just regular margarine," he said pointing at the Lurpak. "It's the expensive stuff."

"It was the only stuff I could find," I answered sounding every bit a surly teenager defending their turf. "There was nothing else in the fridge."

"It's normally on a shelf near the oils, close to the baking section," he belatedly informed me.

What kind of margarine can just sit on a shelf? I wondered. "An unrefrigerated shelf?" I asked, searching for clarification on this barbaric notion.

Not wanting to discuss my failed trip to the supermarket any further, I went with a diversion. "Shall we have a coffee?" I asked picking up the milk.

"Sure, but can I have mine black?" he replied, pointing at the milk carton. "That's buttermilk."

Four, Mothering Like a Dane

Neighbourly Relations

A few weeks later, rhythmic bangs vibrating from somewhere above my head jolted me awake. The ceiling lamp alarmingly swung in time with the pounding from above. *It's not? Is it?* I asked myself, trying to make sense of what had woken me. I was still adjusting to Copenhagen apartment living, including the unexpected sounds that travelled from one apartment to another. *Maybe it's a washing machine? A midnight emergency wash?* I hoped as a squeal of satisfaction projected from somewhere beyond the walls of our apartment, destroying my optimistic laundry theory.

Seeking shelter from the intensifying banging I stuffed my head under the square-shaped pillow, another quirk of European life I'd yet to fall in love with. *Finally, a good use for this abnormally shaped pillow,* I thought as I scrunched my eyes shut, hoping it would stop the mental image that was insistent on banging its way into my head. I prayed the pillow would muffle the neighbourly relations, which if the acoustics were to be believed were happening just metres above my head. I allowed myself a moment of distraction to reminisce about the rectangle-shaped pillows I'd left behind in

New Zealand. *Why would one even think of designing a pillow with a different shape?*

From under my pillow, I could hear my bed companion breathing. Steady breaths, occasionally punctuated with the odd snore. He could sleep through anything and seemed unperturbed by the hide-the-sausage shenanigans happening above our heads. The only other time I'd woken to wild noises on the other side of my ceiling was in a holiday home in Martinborough – a small rural town in New Zealand that had fashioned itself as a vineyard vacation destination. Back then, the owner of the house had shot the perpetrator dead, a possum. *That's probably not going to be an option here,* I thought with a sigh as the banging increased in a climaxing composition. The urgency unequivocally confirmed the thumps were definitely not related to the spin cycle of a washing machine, or a family of possums. *Apartment life.* I sighed slowly as I contemplated my residential fate, making a mental note to buy earplugs when I next braved the outside world.

A Six Pack of Mothers

The next morning I found myself in the middle of an unexpectedly uncomfortable conversation.

"No. It's not possible. They'll find it awkward having you in the group," the baby nurse pointed out with more directness than I imagined our GPS system was capable of. "The Danish mothers won't want to speak English to you," she continued firing her thoughts down the phone line, leaving me as confused as an unpickled herring at Christmas. "Besides, you have your own foreign mother group."

It was true. I'd been assigned into an international mothers' group, but I wanted to meet the locals and had decided Danish mothers would be a better resource for navigating mothering in Vikingland. The previous night's baby-making noises had reminded me I needed to make this call, something I was now regretting as our conversation's 'awkward-o-meter' kept increasing. I detested the foreign label almost as much as the time-consuming flatbed toaster that I was now standing impatiently next to, willing my lonesome piece of toast to turn brown as I cradled the phone under my chin. It was my second attempt to make toast on the ridiculous contraption this morning. The first piece turning an alarming shade of charcoal as I struggled to work out the settings. *Why would anyone have a flatbed toaster these days?* I wondered as I added pop-up toaster to my shopping list of life-enhancing aids I still needed to source.

The awkwardness of our conversation had me wishing I'd used this time instead for my regular morning Skype session with Mum. The 12-hour time difference between the two countries allowed us to share breakfast and dinner catch ups.

"So?"

Snapping back to the matter at hand I realised the baby nurse was waiting for an answer from me. "Sorry," I stumbled in a belated response to her, trying to work out how to respond to her blanket refusal to introduce me to the local mothers in my neighbourhood. The Dane had left for work before dawn, so I wasn't able to throw the phone at him to get me out of the pickle, something I had a bad habit of doing. I had to persevere this time. BBB was thankfully oblivious to the tense negotiations, happily bum shuffling her way around her playmat while I persisted in the standoff with the baby nurse.

"Well, maybe you could just tell them I exist? Let them know I'm here if they want to meet for a coffee?" I asked trying to match her razor-sharp communication style with my own directness. "And give them my phone number?" I half-heartedly suggested as my bravado started to wane and I began questioning just how much I wanted to meet the local Viking mothers. I hadn't anticipated this unexpectedly difficult conversation. I tried to find a way to exit the call.

Mothers groups *(mødregrupper)* in Denmark appeared to rival organised crime squads with their inner workings and implied understanding of how things worked. These groups were responsible for the six packs of mothers I'd seen pushing prams the size of small tractors through parks and visiting cafes en masse as they gathered for their weekly catch ups. I saw them all the time during my companionless walks with BBB, and jealously watched from a distance. They all seemed very happy and connected. I'd yet to make any friends, not that I'd had any time to devote to the task. So, when I did realise these gaggles of Mamas and Bubs were actually forced friendship groups, I enjoyed a small moment of smugness. They were an arranged six pack of mothers, matched by a nameless baby nurse. Their social circles were probably not much wider than mine — in the mothering department at least. But what I hadn't yet worked out was, for a country with incredibly progressive parental leave laws, why weren't Dads part of these groups?

As a new mother in Copenhagen, you'll be allocated to a group of strangers who shall (in theory) be your support group going forward. These groups are normally made up of between four to six mothers who live near you and who you might or might not click with.

"Ok. I'll try," the baby nurse reluctantly agreed before promptly disconnecting my call.

Good lord. It felt like I was trying to bribe my way into university admissions.

Eyebrow Raising

Picking BBB up from the floor, I resigned myself to eating a semi-toasted piece of bread for breakfast while I shovelled some baby porridge towards her mouth. After procrastinating for many weeks, I was finally feeling confident enough to achieve some of the tasks on my get-shit-sorted list. At the top of the list was signing her up for *vuggestue* (daycare) a task I was apparently already three months behind schedule with. Then I really needed to find a beautician to reinstate my eyebrows and a hairdresser that could handle my alarmingly thick non-Scandinavian locks. With The Dane back at work, I was doing my best to master the art of filling in the weeks at home with our daughter. She didn't seem half as challenged as I with our new environment so long as she was fed and changed at the appropriate intervals.

Monday mornings were scaring the bejeebers out of me though. The realisation I had five days of diddly squat to fill in before the weekend when the tempo of the house would change. Walking the streets had become the main activity to fill in the time I might have otherwise spent having coffee with friends, if I had any. I got to check out the neighbourhood while blending in like a local, safe in the knowledge that no one ever stopped and talked to a stranger here. I may as well have been invisible on the streets – which as a foreigner that didn't speak Danish, suited me fine. Fortunately, the streets were also BBB's preferred place to sleep, so long as I kept the pram moving. Unlike her peers that were parked outside shops and cafes, she had yet to work out how to sleep in a stationary pram.

Pushing her pram while she dozed, I double backed past the beauty salon for the third time, wondering if anyone had noticed me circling like a shark. Past experience had taught me that beauticians on the main street were never the ones to go to – they had high prices and attracted less-experienced staff. If you wanted a good beautician, it was better to find the ones off the beaten path. The good ones never had to have a high traffic location to attract customers. Their reputation was all the advertising they needed. It was this theory that had led me to a small beauty studio not far from our home. At a distance it looked decent enough, even if they had used an overwhelmingly amount of shocking pink paint on the billboard hanging above the main entrance. But I still wanted to check out the inside, to get a feel for the clinic before I committed. Today was the day I'd breach their threshold in the hope a sneaky look inside might confirm whether or not I'd entrust my fair-haired brows with them. Swinging open the door, I squeezed BBB and her pram inside the tightly packed reception area.

The Danes have two names for the contraption with four wheels that they move their smallest people around in. Maybe you would have called it a pram, stroller, pushchair or buggy? In Denmark it's called either a *barnevogn* or *klapvogn*. *Barnevogn* is the flatbed variety for newborns. When the babies get a bit bigger and can sit up then they use a *klapvogn*, which is more like a stroller. And me? I call the whole lot of them prams, irrespective of flatbed functionality.

"*Hej og velkommen!*" a breezy young thing greeted me as she welcomed me into the clinic.

"Hello," I slowly replied, giving her a moment to register I was speaking English. "Can I make an appointment for my eyebrows and lashes?" I asked deciding I'd just cancel the appointment later if I had any doubts during this reconnaissance trip.

"Okay," she replied, equally slowly, making me wonder if I'd overdone it and she now thought I had a speech impediment.

"What colour do you normally use?" she questioned.

"Brown," I replied, unsure what that mattered right now.

"We'll need to put some grey with the brown to make sure they don't go green," she replied staring at my locks. "Because of your red hair."

Green? A couple of my closest friends were beauticians and neither had ever shared this alarming risk with me before. *Maybe they have a different brand of eyebrow dye in this part of the world?* I guessed, trying to make sense of why I was at risk of Shrek-themed facial features. Murmurous noises began from within BBB's pram as if she was also protesting the thought of having a mother with green eyebrows.

"Errr. Sure," I agreed out of politeness, unsure what else to say. "Have you got time next week?"

And within seconds I was booked in for a set of either green or grey eyebrows. Reversing BBB from the shop, we headed to our final port of call for the morning outing as my temples began throbbing.

The Drug Run

A short while later I found myself walking around *Føtex*. It was one of the larger supermarkets that stocked a more diverse range of goods. *It shouldn't be this hard to find a box of Panadol,* or *Panodil* as it was called in this part of the world. After five zig zagging loops of desperation through the beauty aisles, I decided to give up, resisting the urge to dial The Dane for help. BBB was due for her next feed soon and I wanted to be home for that. I'd just search again in the bottom of my handbag in case there was still some New Zealand Panadol lurking there. I headed towards one of the self-service checkouts, my preferred option for going incognito. Another string of articles over the last week about tightening immigration policies had me trying to hide my foreigner-ness even more than normal. The most memorable headline this week had been 'Axe-wielding clown chases Dane'. *Would it have been a lesser crime had it been a foreigner? Or were they implying the clown was a foreigner?* I'd wondered slightly uneasily.

I threw my bag of oranges onto the scales and realised I had no idea what they were called in Danish. Such was the audaciousness of Vikings they'd renamed the one fruit that was self-explanatory. I began searching through the list of fruit and vegetables, hoping to crack the citrus code when *appelsin* opportunely flashed up.

Apotek is the Danish word for pharmacy and where you'll find the largest selection of over-the-counter drugs. Although, even at an apotek you'll still have to chat with the pharmacist before taking any cough medicine, of which the choice is limited.
Additionally, in an attempt to reduce the number of attempted suicides and deaths due to the incorrect use and/or dosing of *Panodil*, the highest quantity that can be bought of these tablets without prescription is 20.

Pushing past a small group of people all checking their supermarket receipts for reasons I didn't understand, I headed home with BBB. If I was still feeling courageous when I got home, I'd start ringing some of the local *vuggestuer* to begin the daycare search for **BBB**.

Danes are generally trustworthy. Really trustworthy. It's a trait lauded in most articles written by Danish commentators. Although, there are two exceptions. **Number one.** Arla milk crates. These bright-green and very sturdy milk crates are stolen in staggering quantities throughout the country. After which they are repurposed for numerous things including kindergarten play equipment and bike baskets – they've even been spotted propping up cars (after their tyres have been stolen). On average, the milk giant of Denmark, Arla, loses 300,000 milk crates every year.

Number two. Supermarket pricing. Always check your supermarket receipts in Denmark. There are a couple of supermarkets with a notorious reputation of advertising special prices but not making the necessary changes within their computer system. Which is why you'll see many a Dane hovering at the end of a supermarket conveyer belt double checking their receipt like it were a bingo ticket. They're making sure the shelf price matched the till price.

Five, Integrating With Danes

Blogging Along

Closing my eyes a few months later, I hit 'Publish' while at the same time hoping the Wi-Fi connection would fail. *I'm probably just another angry foreigner,* I told myself, *maybe I shouldn't post it.*

Using my fingers to pry my eyes open, my blog screamed back at me from the screen in its full alien angst.

To survive or thrive in Denmark

The word 'LIVE' flashed underneath my shouty title in scary capital letters, telling me it was now too late to wish for a national meltdown of the broadband network. The herring had hit the rye bread; the horse had bolted. My blog was dancing free-range in cyberland.

'I've heard it all before,' came the first reply from a name I recognised as one of the leading serial keyboard warriors on all matters expat in the land of pastries. A prolific commentator I always tried to mute. The speed of the reply today confirmed he hadn't looked past the title before the urge to type something overcame him. Ignoring the comment, I hit 'Refresh' again.

I'd been mulling over my thoughts for a few months, trying to articulate my new life as a foreigner with a nagging and possibly imaginary concern I'd be kicked out of the country for expressing them. My family reunification residence permit felt very delicate in an Oliver-begging-for-food kind of way – even if my living-in-sin status made little difference to the government officials. Danes didn't seem bothered with those technicalities; marital status was as much of a non-issue as nudity. It was my non-EU passport that made integrating in Denmark irksome and left me feeling vulnerable after realising my made-in-New-Zealand daughter had lifetime access to Denmark, but I didn't. I was becoming acutely aware my residence permit was like a library book on loan – one that could be recalled at any moment.

Non-EU nationals who are partners of Danes must jump through many hoops to live in Denmark. The first being they need to (in 2021) outlay more than 100,000 Danish kroner (that's about €13,400). The foreign national must then pass language exams within certain timeframes for the temporary residence permit to be extended.

Staring at my black and white diatribe on my screen, a weight lifted from my shoulders, replaced quickly by a fistful of nerves churning in my gut. The fear of feral keyboard warriors pulling my post to bits like a pack of Rottweilers was terrifying. Puffing out my chest in my best display of peacock pride, I primed myself to bat away the next hounding comment.

A New Zealand bestie (not that I had any Danish ones) had suggested I start the blog. A fount of precise advice, Nikki had delicately suggested: "It'll be a good way to add structure to your days – besides you're also quite good at it." Her matter-of-fact flattery worked almost immediately as I scrambled to pick the best platform before launching my *Bilingual Backpack Baby* blog. A few months after launching it, I doubted there were more than a handful of people reading it, something my analytics backed up. *Is this the one to go viral?* I asked myself while trying to work out whether the idea of going viral made me nervous or excited. *Probably not,* I decided, refusing to give any more oxygen to that thought. *The only social media storm I'm going to whip up here is one in my own teacup.*

"What are you doing?" The Dane asked returning from BBB's bedroom after successfully wrestling her to sleep.

I sat at our new glossy-topped dining room table, my back to an alarmingly bright green wall that had somehow been approved during the renovation phase. Even now as I thought about it, sleep deprivation was the only reason I had for how I'd agreed on the paint colour in the first place. It continued to amuse me how I'd moved in with the only Dane in Denmark who hated the otherwise popular virgin white walls prevalent in this neck of the woods. The theory of white walls with pops of colour had been turned on its head in our apartment. Every morning when I sat down for breakfast and stared at the wall, I asked myself what had gone wrong.

"Spilling my guts on the conspiracy of Denmark," I replied.

"What?"

Too direct, I reminded myself. *The Dane was fluent in English but not in my sarcastic ways.*

"I just finished my blog about integrating and finding work in Denmark," I explained, not convinced he fully understood the struggle of my first few months in his homeland. My half-hearted exploration of the Danish job market had so far resulted in all my applications disappearing into black recruitment holes. 'Everyone uses LinkedIn,' he'd told me when I asked how people found jobs in Denmark.

"But I've got lots of international colleagues," he replied unhelpfully. "They don't have any problems finding work."

"You're an engineer," I interrupted in my best monotone, already exhausted before having to explain it one more time. "Every engineer in the world has international colleagues. They could find work anywhere. You're in demand."

"Hmm," came the response.

Even though my search had just begun, finding a job in Denmark already felt like a game of Whack-A-Mole. Constantly being thumped on the head with a hammer until you're out of sight, only increasing in intensity with each blow.

It'd been cathartic to write the blog. Sharing my thoughts on paper diffused some of the blows and helped make more sense of them as I tried to work out the job and social scene in this land of supposed happiness.

"Why don't you get a job as a cleaner?" The Dane adventurously offered.

Placing my cup of tea on the table, I gripped my hands together, resisting the urge to find my own hammer to whack him with. Although to be fair, I did have 10 years of cleaning experience, and I was quite good at it. My very first job had been cleaning school classrooms and it made me one of the highest-paid 13-year-olds at the time. It was an important job, but after 10 years' service I'd hoped my time on the mop had come to an end.

He's just trying to be helpful, I reminded myself before discarding his suggestion entirely. "I'm not the only one struggling. Even Danes can be out of work for a year or longer before they find a job," I replied, repeating a conversation I'd read on the same expat forum where I'd just posted my blog (a page I was spending too much time on). However, the difference for the Danes was they were entitled to financial help from the government or received *A-kasse* (a type of unemployment insurance) while they searched for a job. My non-EU and newly arrived status so far had me on the outer here too.

Glancing back at my screen the red notifications started popping up. Either Mum had sent my blog on to her friends or the local expats' Facebook page was beginning to trigger. Too scared to look, I shut my laptop and slid it across the dining room table. *Forget it. Leave it to the universe,* I told myself as I headed to the sofa with my cup of tea.

Commonwealth-influenced tea drinkers may struggle in Denmark. Coffee is the assumed drink of many social situations and dominates the supermarket hot beverage section. To secure yourself a decent supply of tea bags, hunt out your local Turkish or Afghan independent supermarket. Here you'll find bulk packs of the black-leafed goodness at a fraction of the price in the main supermarkets.

A few days later, waking with a small knot of anxiety in my stomach for reasons that weren't immediately obvious to me, I squinted at the clock. 6.07am flashed back at me. All was quiet. The Dane's single duvet was folded neatly next to me on his side of the bed, telling me he'd already left for the day. *To an outsider we must look like we're on the verge of divorce,* I thought as I considered the anti-social Danish duvet system I was learning to adapt to. A baby snort from the room next door warned me BBB was also beginning to rustle from her slumber.

Searching like a blind octopus, I rolled over, my arms outstretched in search of my phone I'd placed on the uninspirational-yet-perfectly-functional IKEA bedside table. *Once I find a job maybe we can invest in a bit more* hyggeligt *furniture?*

Beyond the walls of our Scandi Sameville apartment, my phone was my lifeline to the world. This brief moment in the morning was my favourite as I scanned for messages from friends and family in New Zealand. The 12-hour time difference between the two countries was ideal. Friends and family often sent messages or discovered my daily Instagram post while I slept, giving me a screen of notifications to wake to.

Scrolling through the list of messages, I nearly missed one from the Ministry of Foreign Affairs, summoning me for a meeting to discuss my integration plan. I'd signed an Integration Contract in the first few hazy weeks of arriving in Vikingland but hadn't paid it much attention because a large part of it was only written in Danish. Which they at least apologised for, before telling me to 'just sign it anyway' in a bold assumption I'd already jumped on the much talked about Danish Trust bandwagon. But as for an integration plan, that wasn't ringing any bells.

Danes have a high level of trust in the government (bar the one time in 2020 when they ordered 17 million minks to be killed). But minks (and green plastic milk crates) aside, in Vikingland you'll often come across small stalls with honesty boxes (including payment options via your mobile phone) where you're expected to pay for what you take. And most people do. At least more often than in other nations.

Sitting up in bed, I stopped scrolling while I willed my second eye to open to be sure of what I was reading. *Gah. They must have seen my blog.* I thought in horror as an image of being escorted to the airport in handcuffs flashed before me.

I shot a message to my New Zealand Bestie. It'd been her suggestion to start the blog, so if I was going down for it, she could come along for the ride.

> Nikki, do you think they've read it?
> Maybe?

She offered this as way of an answer that did nothing to calm the knot forming in the pit of my stomach. The cursor began to twitch again as she continued typing.

> Guess you'll find out when you go to the appointment?

Viking Interrogations

A week later I parked my bike outside the *Jobcenter*, whose Danish name was delightfully similar to the UK English spelling. The building was a predictable four-storey mash of bricks with the same, square glass windows that dominated so many Copenhagen buildings. From the outside it was impossible to tell what lay inside. A gaggle of cigarette sucking 20-something-year-olds surrounded the entrance, one of them tossing their butt as I walked past. It joined the small mountain of cigarette butts already lying on the pavement, filling every crack of the cobblestones. Famed for their beauty – unless filled with tobacco turds. Their old-fashioned charms were wasted on me; their unevenness wrought havoc with my dodgy knee. The wonky stones were shit to walk on. *For the love of asphalt,*

I wondered. *Why so many cobblestones? And why all the smokers?* I made a mental note to add the queries to my evening debrief with my Danish half.

Pulling out my printed appointment letter, I checked the details before pushing my way through the cloud of smoke. I quickly stepped between two heavy revolving doors that unceremoniously spat me out on the other side. The cigarette smoke still lingering on my clothes as I entered the building. Brushing at my jacket in a sad attempt to shift the smell of tobacco, it took me a minute to gain my bearings. Pulling my cycle helmet clear of the door I took a step to the right, narrowly avoiding being swallowed whole again and deposited back outside into Puff the Magic Dragon's world.

Nervously, as if I expected my residence permit to be revoked at any moment, I looked up in search of some directional signage. A bearded bouncer stared back at me, his face expressionless.

Leaning on the reception desk with his heavily tattooed arms, Bearded Bouncer looked like he'd have been more at home at a *Bodega*, as the locals called them. They were the small and dank drinking establishments that I'd not been brave enough to enter, not even for research purposes. The collar of his black shirt was turned up. He chatted to the receptionist, showing her something on his phone as he swiped furiously up, his other hand resting in his top trouser pocket. He was doing a commendable job of blanking me. With the nerves of a teenager trying to get into the local bar with fake ID, I scanned the empty seats in the reception area. Bearded Bouncer looked me up and down before nodding his head in the direction of his companion, the receptionist. Taking the hint I moved towards her.

"I have an appointment at ten," I announced, doing my best to sound confident as I slipped the meeting summons across the tall, white desk to her. My arms struggled to meet her telescopic reach. *Why would they build a desk so high?* I wondered.

"Yellow card?" she said without looking up.

Digging in my wallet, I searched for my precious yellow card that proved my Vikingland legitimacy. Printed with all my important details, including my insanely important CPR (Central Persons Register) number that had my birthdate embedded in it for all to see. It also had my middle name, a name I never used in New Zealand but one the Danes continued splashing about. Another oddity to yet make sense of.

Looking up from his smartphone, the security guard's eyes grazed my 5ft 4in frame as I stood on tippy toes to fling my card across the desk in the hope it landed somewhere close to the receptionist. Viking-sized reception desk aside, the process made me feel as small as Thumbelina in a pub.

"That way. Room 3108," the receptionist replied with all the enthusiasm of a mannequin as she slid my yellow card of life back to me.

"*Tak*," I whispered, thanking her in my primitive Danish, hoping she'd note it as a positive sign of cultural onboarding.

Those arriving in Denmark on a family reunification permit must sign an integration contract known in Danish as an *integrationskontrakt* including a 'Declaration on integration and active citizenship' promising your commitment to Danish society. This includes a promise to ensure your child 'does his/her homework through their school years' and that you understand circumcision of girls is punishable in Denmark.

Ten minutes and two stairwells later I arrived at room 3108. Chairs resembling mini prison cells lined the waiting room, their back and sides towered over my head. Hesitantly I sat down and was immediately swallowed by the chair. My previous high regard for Danish-designed furniture crumbled as my view became restricted to those who walked directly in front of my chair-chamber. *Clever,* I thought to myself, *even the waiting room is designed to make you feel like a criminal.* It was impossible to know how many others were sitting in the waiting room with me. Trying to pretend I was comfortable, I mentally prepared for the inquisition as I waited for my *integrationskonsulent* to appear. Another Danish word that was almost identical to its English counterpart. *Interrogation Consultant would, however, also be quite apt,* I thought.

A stream of tracksuit-clad and backwards-baseball-cap-wearing job seekers sauntered past. I recognised some of them from the tobacco-tossing group at the entrance. Like marching ants, each filled the frame of my chair-prison for a second before disappearing. Popping my head up like a meercat, I strained to see where they were going before returning my attention to my phone, mindlessly scrolling as I waited for my number to be called. Small beads of sweat collected in my palms. *Could they revoke my residence permit because of a blog?* I wondered.

"Shall we do this in Danish or English?" the younger-than-me Viking interrogator began. Her long whimsical dress confirmed the, as I'd named it, 'floaty floral session' of Denmark had begun. Swarms of women in similar full-length flowery numbers were currently filling the streets of Copenhagen as the seasons changed to warmer weather. The more experienced effortlessly matched their frocks to their bikes. I was fairly sure that, if I wore one, I'd not only look like an Oompa-Loompa attacked by a field of wildflowers but it'd also be wrapped around the spokes of my bike wheels faster than a Dane could chuck a Tuborg beer down their gullet. *Or maybe it was an age thing? Maybe these frocks were only supposed to be worn by the young?*

The interrogator's floaty floral number momentarily distracted me from the ridiculousness of her question. *When did she think I was going to achieve Danish fluency?* I wondered as a replay of the last few months rushed through my head. My biggest concern since arriving in Denmark with a four-month-old baby was ensuring, despite my baby daze, that I had clothes on that weren't inside out.

In fear of being turfed out of the country, I shut my internal voice down and instead tried my best to remove the whiff of snippiness from my reply, which was bubbling within.

"English, please."

"So," she began, her eyes distracted somewhere within the white folder in front of her. "Why don't you have a job yet?"

Shit. I thought, sucking in some air. *She makes the average Dane's directness seem saintly.*

"I have a baby," I hesitantly offered by way of the best explanation I could manage. A patch of dried milk on my shirt caught my attention as I lowered my head, hoping to deflect the next missive.

"I see. It will be hard."

Cheery wee thing, I mused more confidently than my insides were feeling.

"What will you do in Denmark? Do you have a degree?" she asked, while continuing to flip incessantly through the white folder in front of her.

I'd been through all these questions when I first arrived in Denmark. *What's her game?* I wondered but dared not question, keeping my mouth firmly shut.

"Just a bachelor's degree?" she asked, the disappointment confusingly hanging audibly between us for reasons I didn't understand.

"Yes," I replied as I tried to guess what her point was. To my mind only students who couldn't find a job after gaining their bachelor's went back and did a master's. It was something to fill in their time and we tongue in cheek called them 'Professional students'.

"Yes, this is going to be tough. What is your plan? What job will you do in Denmark?" she repeated, her pen hovering in anticipation of capturing my reply.

Guessing I had about 20 years' work experience on the Viking Interrogator, I wondered if that was the reason for her incessant and disproportionate interest in my university degree. I hadn't given my university degree much thought after graduating. I wasn't sure it'd ever really taught me how to do a job, and I'd got it a lifetime ago. At this point in my life it was merely a certificate, and one I realised I wasn't even sure where the original was. I decided not to horrify her by sharing that – or the fact that I'd gone to university in a time before smartphones and laptops – for fear it would discredit my degree altogether.

University is free in Denmark and students are also paid a comfortable allowance. This is known as SU (*Statens Uddannelsesstøtte*) or State Educational Grant.
A master's degree (four years) is considered by many to be the minimum level of education to have.

The integration audit continued with a seemingly endless list of terrifyingly personal questions regarding my future intentions. Feeling like an overwhelmed first-grader on their first day of school, I slunk lower into my chair. I gripped my notebook with sweat-soaked hands as I digested the news of my multiple weaknesses. Any confidence I'd had in navigating the Danish job market was now firmly squashed out of me, which unexpectedly caused a giant wave of FOMO on experiencing Danish workplaces. Stories from

The Dane's workplace of Friday breakfasts, cakes and mini-flagpoles that popped up with the Danish flag to celebrate his colleagues' birthdays had me intrigued and enthusiastic to join. Mainly from an entertainment point of view, I desperately wanted a slice of the Danish workplace sorority club. The Dane had even told me they sometimes sang. *SANG!* I desperately longed to experience these cultural curiosities myself. But nothing on my workplace wishlist seemed entirely appropriate to share with my current Interrogator, who was adding another note to her file.

"What job do you want? We need to make a plan," she informed me with the determination and intimacy of a mating praying mantis.

Was my desire to leave the house everyday a big enough motivation? I wondered. As gratifying as it was to nod and smile at the supermarket cashier in Netto, it would be nice to talk to someone other than myself or BBB during the day. *The money would also be useful to buy pastries.*

"People management," I replied, as I watched her write *Human Resources* in my *integrationsplan*. Opening my mouth to correct her, I quickly shut it again like The Cowardly Lion, and instead prayed for a quick release from her den.

How odd, I thought as I walked out clasping my integration plan 10 minutes later, *she didn't even say a word about my blog.*

Navigating home on my bike, I was hit with an epiphany of a pastry. It continued to happen with alarming frequency of late. I took solace in the fact Dad would have at least been supportive of my smoko selections. Alone on my bike my eyes were watering again thinking of him, wishing I could send him a quick message with a photo of the pastry I was about to eat. I was thankful for my sunglasses as the buried grief began bubbling up again, not that anyone on the street was taking the least bit of interest in me. Taking a hard right, I deviated to the Starbucks of Danish bakeries aptly named the layer cake house, *Lagkagehuset*, to cleanse myself of the interrogation. *This isn't going to end well,* I thought as I perched on a stool, pastry in hand, and considered how much more give was left in my stretchy jeans.

The 'H' Word

Emitting an inaudible arrival with an undeniably antisocial odour, BBB timed her delivery at the same time the apartment doorbell rang. *That'll be a Code Brown,* I thought, buzzing the downstairs door open for The Dane to come up before unlocking the apartment door, saving him the hassle of finding his key. I took a quick gulp of fresh air and whisked BBB to the bathroom for a nappy change. This Code Brown wasn't waiting for anyone.

Five minutes later, after a slightly more challenging change, we re-emerged into the living room with a more neutral scent now emitting from BBB's rear end. Standing in front of me was The Dane, still clutching his bag. Surrounding him in a crescent-shaped formation were three Mormons. Their black-and-white name badges left no doubt of their religious mission, but didn't give any explanation why they were standing in our apartment. *Besides didn't they always travel in twos?* Raising my eyebrows in what I hoped was an adequate semaphore fashion to The Dane, I willed an answer from him.

"Who are they?" I whispered, even though in our tightly packed apartment we were standing so close that everyone, Mormons and all, could hear my question.

"I was about to ask you the same. They were waiting at the door when I got home," The Dane replied, smiling at the unexpected group of three next to us, who politely returned our smiles.

Oh feck, I must have buzzed in the Mormons. I thought back to the small groups of people congregating around the door buzzers on the other side of the road when I'd returned from my appointment. *That must have been them.* It seemed impossible the day could get any stranger.

"Ha. Well, that's awkward," I stammered. "I thought you were my husband." I used the 'H' word even though the Dane wasn't my husband – at least not in a marriage certificate kind of way. But now definitely didn't feel the right time to get into the technicalities of our relationship. *Where do the Mormons sit on the whole living in sin thing?* I wondered, as I began side-shuffling the group of three in a crab march towards to the door again.

Perhaps one day I'd be convinced of the need of a bit of a paper to confirm our relationship, especially if the Mormons returned. Until then The Dane was my *kæreste* in Danish –another fiddly-as-a-duck word that remained on the unpronounceable list but did at least sound better than the word 'boyfriend' to confirm he was my other half. At least, it would once I'd mastered how to say it.

Dashing the Mormons' hope of a new sign up, I quickly apologised for the confusion before, much to their disappointment, letting them free onto the street again. I returned to the lounge to a more-relaxed looking husband (of sorts) who'd now managed to put down his bag.

"So how'd it go?" he asked as I returned to the lounge. "Can you stay in the country?"

"Horrible, check this out," I replied, pulling my paperwork from my *Fjällräven* bag. These bags, made to last a lifetime, were an unequivocable sign of Danishness – even if they were a Swedish brand. Buying one had been my early concession to integrating, although unfortunately an act not recorded in my contract with the state.

Grabbing his reading glasses, The Dane gave the document a squinty eyed once-over.

"I can't read it. You'd better check what I agreed to," I continued as I put BBB in the corner to bang Duplo against the wall, briefly considering whether I could do the same but with my head.

"Did they say anything about your blog?" The Dane asked.

"No."

"Well, I guess it was just a normal appointment then," he replied sliding the paperwork back towards me.

"Nothing about today felt normal. Integration feels like a white-washing of my life before Denmark," I replied putting on the kettle. Staring at the water gauge as it boiled, I willed it to keep tempo with my own mood that was bubbling over, while considering how to best navigate having my butt in Denmark but my heart in New Zealand.

Compared to the cost of a takeaway cappuccino, cigarettes are cheap in Denmark.

A study by *Danmarks Naturfredningsforening* (Danish Society for Nature Conservation) in 2019 showed that cigarette butts are one of the most common types of rubbish and accounted for 75% of all types of waste in nature. Many of those butts are also thrown on to the streets every day. Filling the cracks between the cobblestones with alarming speed.

Six, Nothing Like a Dane

Knickers, Knickers, Pants

Squatting over the porcelain bowl with my pants around my ankles, I abruptly came face to face with a grey-haired Viking. It wasn't how I'd imagined the quick pitstop would go when I'd asked The Dane if I could relieve my bladder mid road trip. Grey-haired Viking stood determinedly at the entrance to my toilet cubicle, her right hand still gripping the door handle that moments earlier we'd both vigorously fought over. Holding the other side of the doorframe with her remaining hand, she looked like a starfish bent on blocking my exit. *Not that I'd get very far running away with my pants around my ankles,* I thought to myself. Blinking, to check if this was really happening, I re-opened my eyes to find her still staring at me with all the determination of a deer hunter that'd just cornered their unsuspecting prey. A river of Danish began to flow from her mouth as I considered my options with my pants at half-mast. In an attempt to defend my territory, I scrambled to haul my jeans up while trying not to flash my bits. *The only thing worse than a shouty elderly Viking in my cubicle, would be one dying of shock.* Her Danish sermon increased in volume and tempo as I hastily zipped up my jeans.

So much for Danes being non-confrontational. Grey-haired Viking was in no hurry to wrap up whatever the hell was happening. As she continued, I briefly pondered if it was better to be berated in a language I knew, or one that I didn't.

"Hvorfor er døren ikke låst?" the elderly woman yelled in my direction, presumably asking why my cubicle door wasn't locked.

It was a good question, the door had been difficult to close, but I was more interested in why the Grey-haired Viking, with her pants in their proper place, was so worked up about my door given I was the one in a vulnerable position. *Shouldn't I be the ranty one?* I thought as I mulled the situation over, trying to make sense of this potential cultural misunderstanding. I'd longed for small talk with strangers ever since moving to Denmark, but this wasn't what I had in mind. My vulnerable state rendered me even more mute than normal as I gathered my thoughts.

"Nej," I spat out like a seal protecting its young, relying again on my limited Danish vocabulary to mask my challenged linguistic skills. Grey-haired Viking stopped yelling but continued lingering like a virus at my wide-open cubicle door. Without anything else left in my Danish chit-chat repertoire, I reached over my handbag that was sitting in front of my feet, grabbed the stainless-steel door handle and yanked it shut. It was the only strategy I could come up with under pressure.

"What happened in there?" The Dane asked as I returned to the car, taking my screwed-up nose as a sign of all was not well.

"I had a toilet invader," I replied, giving the short and slightly theatrical version of events.

"Why?"

"No idea. She just whacked opened the door and began yelling at me while I was sitting on the loo."

"No, I mean why didn't you lock your door?" The Dane clarified.

"It wouldn't lock." I defended myself.

"Did you put money in the handle first?"

"No," I replied, confused with the line of questioning.

"They're pay toilets. It'll only lock if you put the money in first." The Dane helpfully explained the inner workings of the railway station toilets, as the chain of events now painfully made some sense. The women before me in the loo had made a big deal about holding the door open for me, ushering me in as she left the cubicle. I thought she was being friendly, not inciting fraud.

"Oh." Was all I could manage in reply as I realised I'd just made a complete tit of myself. *Thank God we're heading to the summerhouse, I need to get away from all things Viking for a bit.*

Hedges, Flags and Beds

Rounding the final corner in the car, the summerhouse came into view. From the corner of my eye I could see The Dane's shoulders begin to knot themselves together. It seemed he'd got his first glimpse of the overgrown, bulky, you-shall-not-see-anything hedge that exploded from the property's perimeter. Now he'd have a long to-do list of jobs before the relaxing part of the holiday could start. I pretended not to notice.

"Dammit. Look at that hedge." He exhaled. BBB responded by beginning to stir as he turned off the car engine. She'd been asleep for most of the trip since the toilet encounter.

"Why don't you just build a fence?" I helpfully suggested. "Then you wouldn't have to go through this every time we come here." *And I wouldn't have to go through it either.*

I'd previously tried convincing him of the benefit of replacing the hedges with a wooden fence. It was unsolicited advice I'd been offering ever since my first visit when the hedges were in their infancy and my future flashed before my face. Fences wouldn't require constant pruning and would give us privacy all year round, avoiding the need to feel like a goldfish in a bowl for the winter months when the leaves disappeared. It was a theory he wasn't having a part of. He was similarly unenthusiastic when I shared my vision of a smooth, asphalt driveway to replace the current gravel one.

"We don't do that here," he replied flatly. "It doesn't look good."

Since when? I wondered as I re-evaluated my relationship with asphalt. Stepping out of the car, I looked along the short, unsealed lane. There wasn't a wooden fence in sight. Every property was encapsulated with a hedge and finished with a gravel or grass driveway. Most were also home to a fully-fledged flagpole.

"But then you wouldn't have to spend your holidays cutting it," I continued campaigning as we unpacked the car. "I read there was more than 200,000 summerhouses in Denmark, that must mean there's at least 100,000km of hedges that needed pruning at least twice a year." I offered after doing some crude calculations in my head and hoping The Dane wouldn't fact check me on them. "Isn't it an inefficient use of time?" I asked. *Unless cutting hedges was considered hygge?*

Cutting hedges is not hygge but does take up a lot of time in Denmark.

"Shall I grab some pastries?" I suggested, applying my top Danish coping strategy to the seemingly stressful situation as I grabbed the last of the bags from the car.

The Dane distracted by assembling the hedge trimmer and his industrial earplugs, offered no response.

Standing back for a moment, he marched onwards, trimmer in hand, towards the frontline to declare early war on the hedge. I headed indoors with the once again sleeping **BBB** in her car seat capsule to make sense of the sleeping arrangements, reluctantly accepting that pastries would have to wait.

The people of Denmark are obsessed, in a firstborn kind of way, with their flag. It's used to celebrate birthdays, anniversaries as well as decorating the Christmas tree. Flagpoles in private yards are a common sight.

The Danish Bedding System

Biffing the duvet covers across the room I briefly considered if we could instead use sleeping bags. Like an octopus with two arms, I'd spent the last 20 minutes trying to coerce not one, but two duvets into their respective covers. They were now taunting me from the floor on the other side of the room, their crumpled appearance evidence of our wrestling match.

If you're going to make suboptimal duvet covers, then the least you could do is have one per bed, I mentally berated whoever was in charge of bed linen in Denmark.

The country's bedding system – based on one-duvet-per-person and not the one-duvet-per-bed system I'd grown up with – was exhausting. For the global kings of all things cosy, I wasn't entirely sure they'd got this one right.

"What's wrong with the duvets?" I yelled at the Dane who had returned indoors.

"What do you mean?" He surveyed the scene with a bemused look on his face as he entered the bedroom.

"They don't fit," I exhaled like a deep-sea diver returning to the surface. I picked up the duvet to show him the excess bunching at the bottom, "See?"

"You've got the 220cm inners, but you're using the 200cm covers," he stated.

The Dane was officially speaking Greek to me. *220? What the hell is that?* Where I came from no one knew the measurements of their duvet, it was either Queen or King. Period.

"Here's the 220s," he said throwing two more duvet covers from the overflowing plastic linen storage box under the bed at me.

"Are they queen sized?" I asked.

"They're 220s," came the unhelpful reply.

Making a bed really shouldn't be this hard. With no fecking idea what 220s were, I decided instead to take a deep breath and channel my inner Inspector Gadget arms as I gave up on any further clarification. Resuming the jigsaw puzzle of matching sheets, duvets and duvet covers, I gave it another shot. Ten minutes later the duvets were dressed – whatever 220s were, it'd worked. I smoothed mine out flat on my side of the bed. The Dane swooped in to fold his in thirds and lay it on top of his side of the bed, like he always did for reasons I didn't understand. But otherwise, the beds were made, the flag was up and the hedge was cut. We were now ready to enjoy our summerhouse holiday. A welcome break from Copenhagen apartment life and the neighbours' rumpy-pumpy sessions. *Next time, I'll see if I can cut the hedge instead,* I decided, plotting ways to avoid another manchester fiasco as I collapsed on top of the bed. My head hit the pillow just as BBB began to wake.

Boobs, Bums and Birthday Suits

"Crikey. Is it a nudist beach?" I asked, looking at The Dane for clarification on the scene in front of us that was unexpectedly confronting my senses. Instinctively, I clutched my towel tighter as we walked over the Scandinavian sand amid a sea of boobs and almost-birthday suits. We were searching for a spot to park our overdressed selves. Trying to act cool amid the sudden onslaught of half-dressed bodies, I sensed my shoulders were awkwardly raised like a prudish flag. Grateful for my dark sunglasses, my eyes darted nervously along the beach in a desperate search for any swimsuit-wearing beach companions. The onslaught of nudity unnerved my conservative Commonwealth genes.

Summerhouses are a big thing in Denmark with around 200,000 throughout the country. Privately owned holiday homes to which the Danes like to run away, at any time of the year (irrespective of their summer themed name). So special that only Danes can buy them, unless you negotiate a special dispensation with the Ministry of Justice.

Noticing my discomfort, The Dane dismissively replied 'they're just kids' as he waved in the direction of two naked mini-Vikings who were re-enacting a wrestling match in the shallow water with great ferocity. It was normal to him of course, which was the reason he was also completely unperturbed with the two fully grown blondes lying topless on the beach on our other side. *They're just airing their boobs,*

I told myself trying to pretend it didn't shock me. Looking down at BBB in her cycle trailer, I took stock of the outfit I'd wrestled onto her body before we left the summerhouse. A pink long-sleeved UV50+ New Zealand-made swimsuit, a big floppy sunhat and one and a half layers of sunblock. "Are we overdressed?" I asked no one in particular, as I reviewed my own ensemble: a full-length wrap-a-round skirt, a sensible t-shirt that covered my shoulders, a wide-brimmed hat and two layers of sunblock. A wave of sun precaution self-consciousness swept over me as I looked for somewhere to hide the UV-protective tent tucked under my arm.

"What's the big deal?" The Dane questioned, staring blankly at me. "They're just boobs and bums."

Well yeah, I thought. *But most of the time boobs and bums are decorated with clothes, aren't they?* "I suppose," I replied, pondering what he meant. Unless I was breast feeding, I knew the chances of me getting my 'girls' out at the beach to fly in the wind were zero – and not least because I feared them slapping some poor unsuspecting beachgoer unconscious. In New Zealand my boobs, along with anything else I unleashed to the sun, would be roasted quicker than a Sunday chicken. Within half an hour they'd turn bright red and stand a good chance of third-degree burns. But ozone hole aside, my prudish, freckled fair-skinned Kiwi DNA struggled to embrace the blasé approach of the Scandinavian nudity currently on display.

"Did you know," The Dane started, "in Finland, families sauna together. Naked?"

Horror rippled through my body and I began counting my blessings for meeting a Dane and not a Finn. Reaching a bend in the beach, we found a small grassy knoll on the edge of the sand and threw down our gear. Erecting my sunshade tent, I checked my phone, calculating when I'd need to apply my next top-up layer of sunblock.

There are no laws prohibiting nudity in open spaces in Denmark. So be prepared, be at one with bums, boobs and (gasp) 'rod' reveals.
Winter bathing is especially loved by the older generation and is often done in one's birthday suit. And should one be lucky enough to reach 70, 80 or 90, then why the hell not indeed.

"Hmm. This is nice," The Dane murmured to himself before laying on his towel in the full sun and preparing to enter his resting Viking pose flat on his back with his eyes shut. He was all business, setting the alarm on his phone to best capture his quota of Vitamin D. Then, with the obedience of a hypnotised cat, he rolled over and fell asleep. Boobs and bums aside, I had to marvel at such Danish efficiency to be able to turn off just like that. While he slept I remained upright watching over the two members of my family while observing the beach and its inhabitants from the safety of my sun shelter.

Squinting from a distance, I considered that it could've been any beach in New Zealand in the 1980s, before the ozone hole appeared in the southern hemisphere and the importance of hiding from the sun was drilled into us. The beach in front of me now was a melanoma convention in the making with multi-striped beach towels spread across the sand, their owners in a range of hues from brown to very brown, all studiously lying flat on their backs in the hope of winning the title of Brownest Legs. Children ran freely in and out of the water, building sandcastles and harassing any signs of crustaceous life they found underneath the rocks.

Noticing my mouth was hanging open in shock over the reckless sun worshipping, I forced it to close. *Didn't they get the same 'Slip, Slop, Slap' memo we had in New Zealand?* I wondered as I remembered the nationwide government campaign that drastically changed Kiwis relationship with the sun. Encouraging them to 'slip' on a t-shirt, 'slop' on some sunblock and 'slap' on a hat.

Unexpectedly, a fully clothed Viking appeared in front of my sun tent. *Thank goodness for small mercies,* I thought. *A less-dressed person could have poked an eye out at this angle.*

"*Hej.*"

"Hiiii," I offered slowly in my best Danish accent, as I tried buying some more time to work out who the fully clothed Viking was. *Resist monolingual dumb mode,* I mentally instructed myself.

Crawling out of the sun shelter, I kicked the larger of the two sleeping beauties next to me in the hope he'd wake up and intervene before I turned into a speechless spectator navigating another Danglish conversation. After an obligatory round of handshakes, head nodding and introductions, it was ascertained that the sensibly dressed Viking invader was our summerhouse neighbour. Thankful to not be acquainted with his birthday suit on our first encounter, Sven was sensibly dressed in navy-coloured shorts, which looked almost too good to be wearing at the beach, at least by Kiwi standards. They were matched with a very pink polo shirt. *Bold move,* I thought. There were a lot of men wearing pink in Vikingland. I hadn't worked out yet if it was a Danish thing, or a European thing. Not that I had anything against it, good on them for inserting a bit of rouge in their lives. I watched on as Sven and The Dane entered a conversation that seemed quite serious given the amount of head nodding that was going on.

"Sven and his family are coming over for coffee on Wednesday," The Dane told me. "I did tell you, right?" he said as Sven walked back in the direction of his summerhouse.

"Wednesday? When's that?" My still unemployed status, coupled with the current summer vacation mode, had rendered the days of the weeks meaningless to me.

"In two days"

"Why don't they just pop over when we're home from the beach?" I asked, confused as to why we had to confirm a coffee two days in advance with the neighbours.

"We like to plan," The Dane replied.

Remembering the invitation we'd received two weeks earlier for a 50th Birthday party that was over four months away, I couldn't argue with that observation. I'd snickered my amazement at such forward-planning at the time.

Bringing myself back to the present, I continued marvelling at the formal planning while on holiday too. *Just for the neighbour to pop over for a cup of coffee? Lord save me,* I thought, yearning for a bit more casualness in our social arrangements. *That'll be why giant-sized family wall planners are so popular here,* I thought, imagining them overflowing with entries for Christmas lunches, birthday parties and coffee invites with the neighbours.

Most Danes have a curious habit of arranging social invitations well in advance of the actual event. To manage these long-range social interactions one would be well placed to invest in a giant family sized wall calendar.

Bonus insight: Weeks in Denmark begin on a Monday and end on a Sunday, which may seem logical, but not to everyone.

The Flag Police

Later that day, safely back at the summerhouse we settled ourselves in the garden to enjoy the rest of the unseasonal heatwave.

"Is that that the Norwegian flag?" a middle-aged woman asked her husband as they walked past. Following behind was a trail of what I presumed were family-related members, reminding me of a herd of different sized elephants crossing the road in a line. I'd noticed these Viking packs of walking groups were especially prevalent in the summerhouse area. I expected they, like me, used walks as an excuse to inspect each other's properties while pretending not to.

We were unintentionally eavesdropping from our hidden vantage point on the other side of the newly pruned hedge, The Dane translating the conversation while we cooled off in our small paddling pool. Unconvinced with our bathing strategy, **BBB** was doing her best to empty the pool with a bucket, and to give her credit she was making good progress as I watched the water level drop slowly. The flagpole, all 8m of it, was a gift for The Dane's 40th birthday. It gave him almost as much enjoyment as it gave me amusement watching him religiously raise the flag every morning and lowering it by 8pm or sunset, whatever came first. It was an important rule to respect.

"No, it's not the Norwegian flag," the male of the pack declared after a moment of consideration, before pausing again and correcting his wife. "It's Australian," he offered while staring up at the New Zealand flag that was flying limply below the ginormous Danish one.

"Ahhhh," sighed his wife in what I took to be impressed tones.

Through a gap in the hedge, I could see the middle-aged wife nod proudly at her husband's extensive flag knowledge. Simultaneously, a ripsnorter of an explosion exited my nasal passages. One of such force I had no hope of catching it. The walking Viking pack, startled by the unexpected explosion from the other side of the hedge, fell silent, quickened their pace and disappeared around the next bend. I'd have to correct their flag folly the next time they passed.

The Dane sat smiling at me in amusement. He knew it was tiresome for me to continually correct others on what the New Zealand flag looked like.

"Well, they are just about the same," he gallantly advised. "Red stars versus white stars, you can see how it happens right?" The New Zealand flag looked like the size of a postage stamp in comparison to the Danish one and lack of wind aside, I was beginning to get suspicious if the Dane had sewn rocks into its seams as I watched it struggle to fly.

Seizing this moment for a cultural lesson, and to no doubt also convince me of the Danish flag's charms, the Dane began explaining its history.

"The Danne what?"

"*Dannebrog*. It's the name of the flag."

They named their flag? I marvelled at the intensity of the Vikings.

As well as being the world's oldest and possibly the easiest to draw, the locals exhibited a deafening affection for the Dannebrog. It was everywhere – the one item I could find without fail at the local supermarket. They came in every size, together with bunting, balloons, cups, plates and napkins. All of which were undeniably and infinitely easier to find than the milk or bloody baking margarine.

In 1219, the Danish flag (which shall now be known as Dannebrog) fell from heaven during a battle in Estonia (of all places) making it the world's oldest flag.

Erupting like toadstools in search of daylight, the flagpoles in our sleepy summerhouse neighbourhood remained my top entertainment source. Observing the ups and downs of the neighbourhood – along with the double-takes at our blasphemous dual-nationality flagpole was a daily delight. I'd proudly claimed us the title of Flagpole Rebels of the neighbourhood for daring to fly an outsider's flag.

"Is it your birthday?" an elderly neighbour had asked The Dane on our last visit to the summerhouse.

"No," he'd replied, unfussed with the inquisition.

"Then why are you flying the flags?" The neighbour enquired, clearly puzzled with our flag antics. "It's not a flag day is it?" he asked, half as a statement and half as a question.

I thought every day was a flag day in Denmark.

The Dane later showed me the cut-out card he'd sellotaped on the inside of our laundry cupboard where the flags (folded meticulously) were stored. On it was a list of all the national flag days that the older generation appeared to pay more attention to than others. The reverse of the card also showed bullet points for good flag etiquette. I had the feeling this was not the kind of fine print to be ignored. If one got this stuff wrong I suspected it could lead to some awkward moments. *This is the stuff they should be putting in mine and every other foreigner's pledge to be a good citizen*, I thought as I wondered if Flag Police was a thing in Denmark.

Denmark has 17 (and counting) official national flag-flying days. Additional flag days are added when the children of the royal household turn 18.

"Well, if yours is called the Dannebrog, what shall we call my flag?" I asked.

"Little One," he dryly replied.

Dingoes, Babies and Burglaries

A few days later a mini dust storm of flour was swirling in the kitchen as I threw down a final handful of flour onto the marbled, kitchen benchtop. BBB had about 20 minutes left of her nap and the neighbours were due in five which, given they were Danes, meant they'd arrive bang on time. That left me four minutes to knead the scones and get them in the oven. I hadn't quite worked out how they did it, always arriving to the minute on time. *Maybe they just hover by the doorbell waiting to ring it at exactly the right time?* Avoiding my floury dust storm, The Dane was wisely sleeping outside, lounging like a lizard on an oversized beanbag in the mid-afternoon sun. It was the hottest summer on record for 100 years' with the locals stripping and sunning themselves in record numbers. I was horrified.

The Dane had entrusted me to prepare the food for our coffee visitors. I'd decided on scones, jam and cream in the hope they'd cope with the foreign offerings. It was one of Dad's favourite smoko options. My new smoko companions, two Danes and their children, was a much higher risk crowd more accustomed to bread, cheese and jam being on offer. *I'd better give them instructions on how to eat them.* Cut, butter, jam, cream and serve. And not, God forbid, how the locals were eating the Scandinavian scone cousin I'd seen in the local bakeries. It was a poor relation made with chocolate and eaten whole like its popular Danish cousin, the *børnebolle*. No knife, no butter, no jam – and as such both deviant and confusing for a Commonwealth baker.

Børnebolle, the magic bun of Denmark, is essentially just a white bread roll, although lighter in texture than your standard white roll. It's an approved form of currency for the bribing of small children, with some bakeries giving them away to children for free.

Washing my hands, I looked over at the convoluted three-dimensional Vitra wall clock. Had it been hanging a bit lower, one could have been forgiven for thinking it was a coat rack with its twelve pointy sticks. The doorbell rang.

"They're here," I yelled at the Dane, who had now returned from his sun worshipping session on the deck. "Right on time too," I commented as I finally made sense of the abstract clock.

"Of course they are," he replied, walking towards the front door non-plussed with the uncanny ability of his countrymen to arrive smack on time. Greeting the sensibly dressed Viking from the beach, Sven, The Dane shook hands and ushered him and his wife inside. Athletic Mette was 6 feet 2 inches, blonde and ridiculously lovely and muscular in equal measure. Even on my tiptoes I only reached up to her armpits. Their two children, Josefine and Magnus, predictably blonde and blue-eyed, trailed behind curiously looking towards the kitchen. Awkwardly for my self-confidence, they were both taller than I. *How is that possible? They can't be more than 12 or 13 years old, tops?* The whole family were benefactors of never-ending Viking legs.

"Sorry, our chairs were stolen," Sven explained as he zeroed in on me with his hand extended, in search of a handshake.

Extending my arm fully and firmly, partly in attempt to defend myself from any impromptu European kissing, I greeted our visitors. "That's okay. You didn't need to bring any chairs, we've got plenty," pointing outside to where The Dane had set up the garden furniture.

"I don't think that's what he meant," The Dane corrected me while the friendly family of four smiled awkwardly at me.

"They took two of our Egg™ Chairs," Sven explained, referencing the famed Danish-designed chair that cost the price of a small car. "Well, they were only replicas, but that never bothers the thieves. We've been on the phone for the last hour trying to sort the insurance."

"Probably across the border by now," The Dane replied with a surprising amount of inside knowledge on burglaries.

The Egg™ Chair was designed by Arne Jacobsen in 1959 for the lobby and reception area of the SAS Royal Hotel in Copenhagen. It is now one of the most iconic Danish designed chairs, as well as a common victim of home burglaries.

"They also took our light fittings," Sven continued.

"They took ours last year," The Dane chimed in, swapping tales of classic Danish burglaries like it was an episode of Sherlock Holmes.

They'd be a bit bloody disappointed in New Zealand, I thought, imagining the thieves look of shock confronted by a La-Z-boy armchair and a ceiling full of downlights. Or worse still a single bulb in the centre of the room. Steering the visitors to the outdoor dining table set with padded red chair cushions, The Dane led the group outside, while I escaped back inside to wake BBB, glad for the excuse to avoid the awkwardness of everyone having to speak English on my behalf.

"Do you like living in Denmark?" Mette asked me as I rejoined the group outside with the scones and coffee.

I always got asked that and every time it made my eyeballs roll into the back of my head. The locals only ever expected a positive reply. Much how I'd expect any visitor to New Zealand to wax lyrical about my country. It was a question that irritated me beyond reason.

"Denmark's a good country," I began, "but so is New Zealand. I'm lucky to have the pick of two of the best, I guess?" I flippantly replied hoping I could distract her with the scones that were now on the table, to take the steam out of her line of enquiry. I hadn't articulated the swirling thoughts in my head about Denmark to myself yet, let alone be able to share that with anyone else. After finishing their scones, courteous Josefine and Magnus chanted in unison 'tak for mad' thanking us for the food. Their plates were empty in a seemingly successful introduction to the foreign food.

"The children want to know what you say in New Zealand when you've finished eating?" Athletic Mette asked, her toned arms glistening as she reached for her coffee.

"Oh. Well, nothing really," I said, trying to think of a typical New Zealand eating scenario. "Well, nothing special at least."

The children looked at me in disbelief as my words were translated for them. Magnus sought confirmation of the barbaric practises via his mother.

"You don't say thank you for the food?" Athletic Mette queried with hints of incredulous tones.

"Well we do, of course we do," *don't we?* I thought. "Well, most do, but it's not as scripted as what you say in Denmark. There's a lot of different things you could say to show you're grateful for the meal. Like 'thanks' or 'thanks for that', for example."

Magnus looked at me with a face that indicated he now believed New Zealanders to be heathens. Even to my own ears this explanation sounded weak.

"Oh, that's different. We always say *'tak for mad'*. What else is different in New Zealand?" Mette asked unprepared for the bombshell I was about to drop.

"Well babies, don't sleep outside," I offered as the most glaring obvious difference – to me at least.

"They don't?" she replied equally incredulous.

Sensing she'd found this a bit wild I braced myself for the inquisition.

"Babies don't sleep outside? Why not?" came the first line of inquiry.

Mentally releasing the internal sigh that was building inside me, I searched for a way to explain that not all babies in the world slept like the mini-Vikings of Denmark and their Scandinavian cousins.

"No, they don't. Well, sometimes they do," I said, confusing my Danish audience immediately. "Well, if the baby falls asleep in the pram during a walk, then it might be left in the backyard, or on the porch until the baby wakes up. But the pram isn't a, ummm, destination bed. You won't see rows of prams outside cafes, shops or movie theatres with sleeping babies in them, like in Copenhagen."

Unrepentant in her quest to learn more about New Zealand, Mette repeated herself in her lovely yet Danishly direct way, "Why not?"

Round two.

"Umm. The weather?" I suggested, while at the same time being acutely aware I was waving a red flag at a bull. Any true Viking would laugh me out of town for using the weather as an excuse for anything.

Placing babies outside to sleep in their prams is a Danish way of life that caused a major international incident in 1997 when a Danish mother tried to do the same while visiting New York. She was arrested (as well as strip searched) for leaving her daughter asleep in her pram outside the restaurant she was eating in. It was a cultural misunderstanding of epic proportions.

Trying my best to explain the ferocity of the frequent 120km/h winds in my home city, which was officially known as 'the windy city', Mette's unimpressed face told me she was having none of it. Attempting again to paint a picture of just how violent the wind was I tried sharing tales of recycling bins and peg buckets flying down the street.

"How cold does it get there?" she asked, pressing me for proof.

"Err. I think it was 2 degrees this morning," I answered, indirectly knowing that I was still going to lose this round. Denmark got colder than that. But not with the same wind chill I reasoned to myself. "Besides, if we left a pram outside in New Zealand, someone would steal it," I claimed, outing my fellow countrymen as bandits.

The gasp of surprise was audible, but short lived. Mette's impatience with my unsatisfactory answers explaining the cultural differences between the two countries started to visibly show.

Placing her coffee cup back on the table with force, she stared into the distance, her eyes narrowing as she considered the situation. "Ahhh," she said, exhaling as if to release her confusion and unfurrowing her brow, which had been scrunched since we began the conversation. "I know why."

Thank goodness, I thought as I sensed the end of the conversation was nearing.

"It's because of the dingoes," she declared, referring to a wild breed of dog with an unfair reputation for stealing babies, that were native to Australia, not New Zealand. Something I refused to let stand in the way from wrapping up this conversation. Fact checks be damned.

"Yes," I said quickly. "That's it. The bloody Dingoes."

Denmark is a land full of people who have signed up to the motto 'there is no such thing as bad weather, just bad clothes'. Something that is repeated until your ears bleed.
Bonus insight: New Zealand does not have Dingoes.

Seven, Speaking Like a Dane

Summer Lovin'

Safely back in Copenhagen, the unwelcome sound of squawking birds, awoke me from a deep sleep. Our escape to the summerhouse was over and now relegated to the memory banks. Rolling over, I squinted at the bedside clock, its luminous red digits flashed angrily back at me. Even the clock seemed to agree it was an obscene time to be woken by wildlife in the middle of the city.

3.52am

Without turning on the bedside lamp, I could see every feature of the bedroom. Even the chair in the far corner – which no one ever sat on but was always strewn with clothes not quite ready for the washing machine – was easily visible. *We may as well sleep with the lights on.* I cursed the never-ending Scandinavian summer light that had been torturing my sleep patterns for the last few weeks. The slumbering Dane lay next to me, oblivious to the chirp-fest taking place in the communal garden below. His dislike for black-out curtains was a bone of contention between us as I tried to accommodate my slumbering practises to the perpetual twilight zone in which I now lived. It felt like someone was holding a giant searchlight a metre from my face, such was the intensity of the light bearing into my eyeballs. Declining my request for proper curtains, he'd instead gifted me an eye mask.

"It'll help," he said optimistically.

Fuck off, I yelled silently to the wilderness ructions beyond our double glazing as I willed the chirping crackerjacks to knock it off. I needed a couple more hours of sleep to fortify myself for my interview at the language school later that day. *Slug gun. I need a slug gun,* I thought in my sleep deprived daze while wondering how I'd become someone with questionable anti-wildlife thoughts. Wishing death upon our feathery friends just beyond our bedroom windows wasn't my normal style. An image of my first childhood pet, unimaginatively named Cocky the Cockatiel, flashed into my head. I'd spent hours trying to teach him to talk, convinced if he knew enough words he could tell me what it was like to live in a cage. Which was kind of how I felt living in Denmark, learning Danish painfully slowly in the hope I might better articulate my caged life. Cocky came to an untimely demise after being accidentally released to the outside world by my uncle who thought he'd like some fresh air. It was an awkward family moment. *But at least he escaped his cage,* I darkly pondered. *What was* my *escape strategy?*

Fumbling in the felt-lined IKEA box on my bedside table I found the familiar plastic cord with an earplug at either end. Squashing them firmly in my ears, I re-adjusted my eye mask and rolled back over, burying my head under my oddly shaped square pillow, something else I was still trying to adapt to. *A chirp fest has got to be better than hearing the neighbours have sex in the garden at least,* I considered, remembering the eye-opening episode a few weeks back. Much like the Viking laying next to me, they hadn't been bothered about the perpetual light either. Light that had illuminated their activities.

Verb Verification

A few hours later, sitting on a wooden bench, it felt like I was waiting outside the school principal's office. Summoned for a misdemeanour I couldn't remember and powerless to stop the impending punishment.

The stainless-steel wall clock was ticking loudly, and was the only thing making any noise in the otherwise deserted corridor, serving only to increase my nervousness. I'd been in a state of self-denial about learning Danish since arriving four months earlier. Not that it wasn't going to happen, it clearly was if I wanted to understand my daughter, and besides the government had listed it on my integration contract as mandatory. So here I was, waiting at the state-funded language school on the hardest wooden benches in all of Copenhagen. The concept of hygge didn't extend, it seemed, to this environment. I reported for the assessment interview, wondering if I'd learn faster than our child. *The kid can't even walk yet. Surely I've got a chance.*

At the summerhouse the previous month, Mette the neighbour had bluntly warned me that Danish was one of the hardest languages to learn in the world. *The world?* I'd thought, failing miserably to mask my dread of starting the journey.

It was 20 years since I'd last been in a school environment and there were literally a hundred other places I could think of where I'd have rather been right then. Already it felt as scratchy as a pair of woollen tights on a warm day.

Arriving at the language school, the lack of English signage had forced me to enlist improvised orienteering skills to find the wooden bench my bum was now parked on – hopefully, in the right place. *Maybe it's the first part of the assessment test,* I thought, pondering my future fate as a foreigner in a land that wasn't mine.

It was a label I continued to hate: 'foreigner'. Continuing to shunt my confidence sideways it made me feel like I had a flashing red sign above my head saying 'not one of us'. As the clock continued taunting me with its painfully loud ticking, I realised it was now 20 minutes past my appointment time. Long enough to challenge my previously held stereotype of Danes being good timekeepers – and to get me nervous if I would make it back home before our daughter needed her next feed. While her father was extremely capable of many household tasks, he didn't possess boobs. Just as I began considering if I could run away, an efficient-looking staff member, clipboard in hand, appeared in front of me. The name written in big black font on the back of her clipboard read 'Mette'.

Good lord – another one.

As of 1st January 2019, there were 38,683 people in Denmark called Mette. It's the third-most popular name in Denmark.

At a quick glance, this one was about a foot shorter than Mette from the summerhouse, but had the same blonde hair. I couldn't help but entertain myself briefly imagining the odds that her surname was either Jensen, Nielsen or Hansen – surnames that seemed to be on every other letterbox.

"Kow-ee?" Academic Mette called loudly while staring at her clipboard. It seemed she was expecting to talk to the masses and not the empty corridor that greeted her.

Oh. Not my turn yet. I thought as I looked along the dimly lit corridor to see if someone else had arrived while I'd been fixated on the stainless-steel clock ticking.

Mette was staring at me.

"Oh. You mean me?" I stumbled to say, as I realised 'Kow-ee' must have been some sort of creative Danish way to pronounce my first name.

"Care-ree?" I clarified, sounding my name out phonetically like a tongue-tied tortoise. "Me?" I asked slowly, pointing at myself like a prized idiot.

Nodding efficiently, Academic Mette tilted her head sharply in an unnerving military demeanour. I took it as a sign to follow her.

"Come," she said, signalling again for me to follow her as she led me past a row of messy, burgundy cubicles drowning in paper to her desk at the back of the room.

Sitting down on one side of the desk, she nodded her head once more at the other side. *I wonder if she gets a sore neck with all that nodding?* Stuffing my cycle helmet under the seat, I took it as my cue to sit.

"You're from Australia?" she asked, not looking up from the form she was beginning to fill in.

"New Zealand," I corrected, trying to be not too judgy, knowing I'd once confused Danish for Dutch and called the Czech Republic Czechoslovakia. They're mistakes you only make once.

"Yes. Australians aren't very good," she continued.

Huh?

"... at learning languages," she clarified. "Australians, New Zealanders, Americans, Brits. You're all the same." Peering over her glasses at me she looked like a woman burdened with the task of telling a child their beloved pet had been run over.

"You're not very good," she elaborated even more slowly while sighing in what I presumed was either forced sympathy or hopelessness with my apparent language learning disability.

"How about we start with something simple?" she asked, handing me a card. "Can you identify the verbs in this sentence?"

I smiled weakly as I did my best to dredge up that knowledge. The last time I'd identified a verb was when I was seven years old. *A noun is a naming word. They both start with 'n', which is why I remember that one. But a verb? It's either a doing or a describing word, but as they both start with 'd' it's not giving me any useful clues to go with.* I had a feeling this task was not going to be quite as easy as Mette was hoping.

"A verb…" I began slowly stalling for time as I looked at the short paragraph written in English. If I couldn't complete this exercise in my mother tongue, then my future prospects at language school weren't looking so rosy. My monolingual language status confirmed that I was embarrassingly and undeniably crap at knowing my adverbs from verbs. Maybe if I knew more one than one language I'd have been in a better position to keep Academic Mette happy, or at the least keep her disapproving stares at bay.

I'd tried and failed to learn a language twice before, something I decided Mette didn't need to know about right now. The first time was as a 13-year-old when I thought German sounded like a useful thing to learn. I lasted for one class before declaring I'd never need to use another language in my life and I'd be better off taking a useful subject – like Shorthand Typing. The second time had been as a final-year university student. Studying only two papers in my last semester, I'd decided to enrol in a French correspondence course to make the most of my time. Every week I received a new cassette tape with my lesson, which held my attention for a little bit longer. I lasted four weeks. I still had no clue what a verb was.

Staring at the exercise she'd given me, unsure what to answer, I was beginning to believe she might be right. *Maybe languages aren't my jam? Maybe I will be crap at learning Danish?* As well as struggling to identify a verb, my brain and tongue were already having minor seizures at the thought of being contorted in directions they'd never been in before.

"Classes don't start again until Week 32. You'll start then," Mette informed me as she continued entering details into her computer while I sat staring into space. I felt like a pauper begging for their next meal, desperate for enlightenment.

Week 32? I thought. "When's Week 32?" I asked in an attempt to bring some light on what seemed like an important subject.

"It's a month after the semester begins, after the summer holidays." She was speaking English, but it may as well have been Japanese. Not wanting to make a fuss I decided to just ask The Dane when I got home.

Heading outside in search of my bike I made a mental note to buy wine on the way home to numb the experience. Turning the corner, I was greeted with a wall of bicycles. During my 60-minute verb verification assault, my bike had been swallowed by a jumbled swarm of kamikaze parked bikes. Mine was now hedged in by a scrum of others, its basket locking horns with its neighbours, proving it impossible to dislodge. I tried pulling it from behind but it was the 'hooker' of the bunch, firmly locked in the centre of a knot of spokes and brake cables. This was worse than a game of Jenga.

Feck. Truly? Why mine?

Giving up all attempts at elegantly removing my bike, I began a rough version of the Copenhagen Shuffle: jiggling the other bikes to the side, one by one, in a bid to extract mine from the pack.

Anywhere is fair game for parking a bike in Copenhagen. There are rules of course: for example, some shops will display signs asking you to not park in front of their windows. But in general people tend to consider anywhere okay to leave their two-wheeled friend.

Bonus insight: It may be Denmark, but it's not Disneyland, so make sure you always lock your bike because bike theft is an ongoing problem. Though it's been on the decline since 2009 with 'only' a little over 45,000 stolen in 2019.

Arriving home, I refrained from throwing my bike down the steep steps into the basement. The steps were on view to the street, enabling our neighbours' front row seats to be entertained with my daily *Bambi on Ice* impersonations as I failed miserably to retrieve and return my bike elegantly from the basement. Others effortlessly wheeled their bikes up and down the concrete ramp one handed, rather than clinging onto it for dear life as I did – yet another thing to master.

Entering our apartment, I began shedding my outer layers. Around the corner I could hear The Dane in the kitchen preparing dinner with BBB at his feet wrestling a toy butterfly.

"How was it?" he asked.

"Okay," I lied, deciding not to share my uselessness at verb identification just yet.

"I start in Week 32. When's that?" I asked.

"It's in Week 32. After Week 31," he unhelpfully informed me while continuing to stir the white sauce in front of him.

I resisted the urge to clobber him over the ears.

"Week 1 is the first week of the year, and week 52 is the last week of the year. And everything else in-between is numbered accordingly," he elaborated.

"And everyone calls them that? It's an official thing? This naming of the weeks?"

"Of course it is," The Dane replied, oblivious that many of us didn't organise our lives by numbers. "It makes sense, doesn't it?"

No. No it doesn't. Not at all.

Looking at the wall calendar I had four weeks until I began my Danish language classes. Hopefully that was going to be enough time to work out what a verb was.

The week system is the habit the majority of Danes use, referring to each week of the year by its number. It makes a lot of sense in a predictable and efficient Danish sort of way, but for those of us who have never referred to weeks by their number, it provides a few challenges. There is no *early August* or *mid-August*, Denmark is a precise land in which it will either be Week 32 or Week 34.

Linguistic Realisations and Limitations

"Do you want a cup of coffee?" I yelled at The Dane, who was sitting on the other side of the room on our 1970s Hans Wegner designed sofa that'd he'd spent the last six months scouring online classifieds for. This and our dining room table were the only pieces of note in an apartment otherwise still lacking the hygge factor.

A short silence followed, interrupted eventually with the now trademark brisk, "Yes." The shock of the missing pleasantry again feeling like a wet fish being slapped across my face. On another day I might have let it wash over me, but the verb verification disaster earlier in the day had left a fistful of blah-ness in my stomach, gnawing at me, causing my shoulders to slump. My resolve was weakened; my immunity to the direct Danish style of communication impaired. Breathing deep, I put out a request to the universe for some metaphorical sugar with his next reply to appease my native English ears.

"Can't you just say it one time?" I pleaded once again in search of the missing reply that would be more soothing for my (possibly) over sensitive ears.

"But you know we don't say please," The Dane replied, speaking on behalf of his fellow country men and women.

Danish furniture designer, Hans Jørgensen Wegner, designed over 500 different chairs earning him the name of the 'King of Chairs'. One hundred were put into mass production helping to turn them into design icons now found in many Danish homes.

"That's why we agreed I'd say it 100 times in the morning. So you can use one whenever you need it later in the day," he reminded me as I placed his coffee in his Royal Copenhagen cup on the kidney-shaped coffee table, which I'd found on the roadside a few weeks earlier. His sentiment of preloading the day with multiple 'pleases' was admirable, but never happened.

Finding free furniture on the street had become a sport in recent weeks, it was an addictive game that gave me a dose of adrenaline in a hunter-gatherer kind of way as I foraged in the urban landscape. It didn't take much to find either, with people regularly placing the things they no longer wanted on the pavement. A lot of it was fully functional furniture – mainly IKEA – that was free for the taking. I just had to be in the right place at the right time to cash in. I'd named my new hobby Danish Dumpster Diving.

With our apartment still looking sparse, this unexpected supply chain was proving to be a successful strategy for tarting things up in our home.

Taking a sip of his coffee, The Dane lurched forward at an alarming speed, spitting it back into the cup. *Charming,* I thought.

"Something wrong?" I enquired.

"Did you empty the kettle first?"

"No?" I replied confused, as The Dane headed towards the kitchen in search for water to rinse his mouth.

"That was descaling liquid in the kettle. Didn't you see the bottle I left by the kettle?" Looking over at the bench, I could see a white bottle with a red lid. *I suppose it did look a bit like a cleaning product?* I observed. *Whatever* afkalker *was?* "Oh right," I answered in non-belligerent tones, ignoring the fact I'd just tried to serve The Dane poison. "Is that the limescale thing?" I asked. The water was hard in Denmark, full of calcium, which deposited itself with alarming frequency in the kettle, with the dregs often making it into the cup. It was not a country to ever take the last mouthful of a cup of tea, unless you wanted a mouthful of limescale and grit. "Sorry. I didn't notice," I offered as I wondered if the universe had confused my previous request for sugar with poison.

The water in Denmark is notoriously hard. Full of chalk, that gathers like bees to a honey pot in your kettle and shower. It will turn your once fluffy towels into cardboard, forever after.

Danish Dumpster Diving

The night before I tried to poison The Dane, he'd bounded excitedly up the stairs after returning from putting the rubbish and recycling out. He'd found a set of Scandinavian designed drawers, albeit IKEA, but nevertheless still very much Scandinavian designed – something we desperately needed for BBB's room. They were sitting next to our small army of recycling bins in the common yard, presumably abandoned by one of our other neighbours.

Last week, he'd found storage baskets for our wardrobe, relieving me not a moment too soon of the pressure of folding and stacking my knickers on the open shelves. Items often appeared after one of us verbalised a need for something. The coincidence was spooky and I couldn't help but be slightly suspicious. Either the universe was on a truly spectacular roll, providing what we needed at the right time, or The Dane was in the midst of a covert operation of robbing our neighbours.

The announcement of his latest find burst from him like a man who'd just won the lottery. "Shall we grab it now?" he offered by way of a plan for the recovery mission as we reconvened in the lounge with non-poisonous coffees in our grip. I noticed the Dane was holding his Royal Copenhagen cup a little tighter than normal.

The communal recycling and rubbish area of Scandi Sameville was a complicated matter. Nothing could be thrown out without first identifying and sorting it. There were separate rubbish/recycling bins for glass, hard plastic, metal, electronics and mixed waste. All labelled in Danish and a tad frightening for someone who didn't know their *pap* (cardboard) from their *papir* (paper). I was finding the whole recycling thing unnecessarily stressful and grey hair inducing, which was altogether a significant feat for a redhead. But the real gem in this multi-bin disposal system was the *storskrald*, the bulky waste. It was there we were heading on this Monday evening while BBB slept.

"You sure she'll be alright?" I asked The Dane, while debating internally if a baby sleeping inside alone was better or worse than a baby sleeping outside on a daily basis in Vikingland.

"Here," he replied throwing the baby alarm monitor at me. "We'll take the monitor. We'll only be 10 minutes."

Grabbing the monitor, I hastily attached it to my shirt like an emergency workers' radio as we headed outside into the dark, cold night to complete our covert operation.

"You're sure we can take them?" I asked looking at the two remarkably good sets of IKEA drawers in front of us.

"Yes. Now come on, it's cold." He ushered me like an unwilling accomplice towards the drawers.

He'd commandeered a wagon with wonky wheels to pull them down the road. "You pull, I'll steer from behind," he shouted as I began frog marching myself down the middle of the road, both arms behind me holding on to the wagons' metal bar, towing it slowly towards our apartment with BBB's first piece of authentic Scandinavian furniture.

Please don't let the neighbours be watching, I thought. *It might not be an illegal activity, but it is a socially awkward one. One I'd prefer no one witnessed.*

Reaching our apartment stairwell in a little less than seven minutes, The Dane swiftly off-loaded the drawers and had them up our stairs and safely in our apartment in record time. His furniture removal efficiency reminded me of the ill-fated Camry road trip I'd taken back in New Zealand with our possessions efficiently wedged into every corner of the car thanks to his undeniable prowess in this domain.

I peeked into BBB's room, a small bundle with both arms flung above her head in the corner of her cot visible in the faint light. She was fast asleep and none the wiser of our late-night shenanigans.

Danes have a wonderful habit of placing what they no longer want, but someone else might need, on the pavement outside their houses. Often in a cardboard box with the simple word *'Gratis'* (free) written on it to indicate you are welcome to help yourself.

The Copenhagen Cough

Cursing their unforgiving steepness, I hauled my bike up the last two concrete basement steps. *Whatever the feck happened to smart Danish design?* I pondered in pain as the rear wheel of the bike swung out, attacking my anklebone. It left a black grease smear as a reminder of who'd won today's battle.

Pushing down on my front mudguard, my wire bike basket sagged heavily under the weight of my textbooks. It was week eight (aka Week 40) of 'Talk Like a Viking' school and my enthusiasm was nearly as low as my bike basket was hanging. Reluctantly heading off on the short 3km journey to school, I said a small prayer to the cycling gods as I made my way down our street hoping I wouldn't piss off the locals while on two wheels. Copenhagen cyclists were brutal.

My silver bell was twinkling like a disco ball, vying for my attention, begging for some action. I was tempted to give in to its demand; it looked awfully quaint. Apart from my Raleigh 20 (circa 1985), it was the first bike I'd owned with a bell. It fascinated and entertained me in equal measure as I attempted to learn when I should ring it.

Rule Number 1 of bike ownership in Denmark: all bikes must be fitted with a bell. The bell should be used when passing other cyclists. However, this rule is overridden by Unofficial Rule Number 2: one should not use the bell unless it's an EMERGENCY.

A swarm of synchronised cyclists swallowed me whole as I turned onto the main cycle highway of Copenhagen, Nørrebrogade, which fed the cycling masses into the city. It was one of many streets I couldn't pronounce. I simply called it the Big Road. The swarm of bikes locked me in like a canned sardine as I held my breath and prayed I'd make it to school without being yelled at by a Viking on a bike. Cycle lanes took precedence over car lanes. Traffic lights were designed in favour of the cyclists on the Big Road. Apprehensively, gripping my handlebars, my knuckles turned white. Enlisting a tried-and-true survival technique, I stuck my tongue out for balance. It was something I'd noticed BBB also did whenever she was concentrating hard to achieve something.

The systematic turning of the pedals caused my mind to drift into a semi meditative state as I wondered what my long-term fate in Denmark might be. *Assuming someday I did master the language, would this country be my forever after home? Could it be?* The majority of my fellow foreigner friends in Vikingland were of the expat variety. Their families' DNA had not been fused with the Viking DNA. They were here for a finite period and their escape route, should it all turn to custard, was a lot cleaner than mine. They were here for a good time not a long time. I wondered if they spent anywhere as long as I did worrying what country their retirement home might be in. *Would I be 85 and still trying to smuggle white bread onto my plate?*

Rugbrød (rye bread) is considered the king of breads in Denmark. It is the Danes' daily bread which, if you're a foreigner, you could be forgiven for thinking was a compulsory requirement for residency. Whereas white bread is seen as more of a treat (or just plain evil by some).

Willing the cycling gods to show me mercy and to avoid the horror of provoking someone to ring their bell or yell at me in Danish, I apprehensively cycled on. A ridiculous state to be in given I'd been riding a bike since I was knee high to a grasshopper. I'd ridden around a mountain and the biggest lake in New Zealand on more than one occasion. In lycra. But all of that accounted for zip right now, as I looked around at the surrounding Vikings on wheels with their baskets and bells. *I can do it,* I told myself as I slipped into a comfortable pace and reminded myself to keep breathing.

Despite the hundreds of pedalling companions around me, the cycle lane was silent, apart from one Cycling Viking on her hands-free mobile kit. *How come she's not puffing while she's talking?* I wondered, marvelling at her mysterious ability to chat while cycling among the Tour de France-like throng. Beginning to relax, an overtaking cyclist abruptly pulled back in front of me. *Uh oh,* I thought as I reached for my bell, unsure if this warranted a ding. *She must have miscalculated my velocity*, I thought. I pulled my fingers away from my shiny bell, chickening out as I debated whether this counted as enough of an infringement to permit a piercing ding-a-ling-ling. I decided to fake cough instead. It seemed politer.

"Ahem," I began.

In public, Copenhageners keep to themselves. There's little small talk, especially with strangers. And even with the thousands of bikes filling the 400+km of cycle lanes across the city every day, they can still be one of the quietest places in Denmark.

The fake cough worked, with the Viking invader veering left, straight into the path of another overtaking cyclist. *Unfortunate timing.* Her handlebars clipped the overtaking cyclist's basket resulting in a flurry of bell ringing and silent hand motions. In slow motion, the Viking invader skidded off her bike. The contents of her basket flew across the cycle lane, bringing all the traffic on two wheels to an abrupt halt. Yet, still no yelling. Looking over my shoulder, I searched for an escape route.

Scooting along the outside of the lane, past the site of the altercation, I decided the best move would be no further intervention from me. Hoping I was an anonymous blur, indistinguishable from the other cyclists in their black jackets, gloves and helmets, I cycled on.

Authoritarian Agnes

Arriving at school after surviving the 3.2km blundering commute, I began bracing myself for the next onslaught. *Here we go,* I thought as Authoritarian Agnes walked into the classroom, an overly zealous briefcase stuffed under her arm, to begin her ritualistic re-arrangement of chairs and tables into her preferred juvenile configuration.

Like a neglected houseplant, my relationship with Authoritarian Agnes was struggling to flourish after being assigned to her class as a result of my verb verification fiasco a month earlier. Her 18th century teaching style pushed my buttons at every touch.

"Du skal sidde her," she advised me, full of the authority of a kindergarten teacher telling me where to sit. It wouldn't have surprised me if she'd tried to lead me there by my ear.

This is going to be painful, I thought. Biting my tongue, I willed my facial muscles to remain neutral and hide the inner disapproval that was threatening to rise up and explode. "Mmm." I gave in and a little snort of disapproval expelled itself from my nose. *Shit,* I cursed under my breath. *For the love of Pete get those snorts under control,* I reprimanded myself.

It was obvious to me we weren't each other's cup of tea and this mutual feeling was unlikely to change. I imagined it was either her disgust at my lack of natural ability to embrace her language, or my age, that unsettled her. Patrolling the class, it was easy to see she was more at ease with the younger and greener students who were, to be honest, a lot more agreeable and pliable than me. Most of them had been lured to Denmark for the free university degree and were now taking advantage of the free language classes for foreigners.

Marching past, Authoritarian Agnes threw today's list of nouns, adjectives and verbs on my desk. *"Værsgo,"* she said shooting a gleeful smirk my way. Her sadistic joy caused my blood pressure to rise and my shoulders to sag with the reminder of how deep the *Dansk* minefield of past, present and plural tense was.

Progress in obtaining Viking bilingualism was difficult to measure. I'd worked out what a verb was, but now failed in the identification of personal pronouns, which I'd had to Google in a break. Like a wicked game of Bluff, I was spending most lessons sitting in a dark language vortex wondering what on earth we were doing. My lustrous young classmates were yet to have their shiny edges rubbed off. Forever obedient and eager to please, their heads moved up and down as one agreeable mass.

Lai Ling was the ringleader of the bobbing squad, a serial front row student. She moved from China for her university education and was now impatiently wanting to master Danish in six months to improve her chances of living in Denmark long term. She was smart, but could also be as annoying as nails down a blackboard. Pushing past that, I decided she might be a good source to decode the classroom schedule of events for me.

"Do you know what we're doing after the break?" I asked her, trying to clarify what the class had just been nodding their heads in agreement at for the last hour.

"I'm not sure," she replied, blowing me off faster than a candle in the wind as she resumed swiping and tapping her phone for her social media fix.

Even the ringleader of the Bobbing Squad doesn't have a clue. I was on a sinking ship with a flock of sheep.

Returning to the classroom, I looked at my fellow students with renewed scepticism. Two Germans, three Chinese, one Swede, a Pole, an American, two Spaniards, an Iranian, a Malaysian and a Finn; most of whom were the other side of 35 to me. An exuberant lot. This was not my learning happy place. *How was I going to prevent The Dane and BBB from conspiring against me in the future if I couldn't get a grip on this?*

Authoritarian Agnes returned from wherever it was that she disappeared to during our mid-morning break, and wiped her whiteboard clean in long methodical sweeps, carefully leaving the day and date at the top of the board.

"Watch the video and we'll discuss," she directed, leaning her pert and perfect behind against her teacher's desk.

Finding the Danish transcript at the back of my textbook, I began following along, trying to make some sense of the strange noises.

Whack. Authoritarian Agnes's hand slammed my book shut sending my drink bottle flying into Lai Ling's lap, momentarily stopping her head from nodding.

Crikey. It'll be the cane next. "Hvad laver du?" (What are you doing?) I asked as my face contorted itself into fully-fledged disapproval mode. *Who even does that? Who slam-dunks a book on a student's desk?* I tried to process what had just happened.

"You must listen to the film," Agnes yelled at me. "It is not right you do that."

Clearly, if your overreaction is anything to go by. I darkly mused as I watched the rest of the film unsure what had just happened.

Sod it, I thought, packing up my books and grabbing my helmet and jacket from the hook on the back wall. *I'm off.* I made my escape while the sea of heads in the classroom continued blindly bobbing as Authoritarian Agnes patrolled her kingdom.

What went wrong? I croaked to myself as I cycled home. I'd never been taught how to learn a language, something I regretted about my New Zealand education but couldn't change. Agnes meanwhile, I surmised, had never learnt how to educate adult students, much less ones that only spoke one language.

"You're home early," The Dane yelled from the kitchen as I attempted to hang my helmet and jacket in the *entré.* It was our small entrance room, which sounded more exotic than the reality and was overflowing with jackets for every season and occasion. *How was it possible for a household of three to have so many jackets?*

The Dane was preparing dinner in the kitchen, as BBB polished our wooden floors with a mixture of dribble and snot. "I think I just dumped my teacher," I replied as I scooped down to pick up BBB for a self-indulgent therapy cuddle. "And I think I'll need to find another one," I declared with all the monolingual bravado I could muster.

Eight, DNA of a Dane

The Great Brown Bread Debate

The rhythmic whirling of The Dane's Kenwood mixer drifted into the office (which also served as the spare room for visitors) from the other end of the apartment. Its monotonous tone interrupted my mindless scrolling of the recent posts in the local expat Facebook group. I'd become hooked on the unexpected drama the group delivered. It was an expat fest of soap-opera proportions. From the Negative Nellies inflicting their miserableness on everyone, to the boring but benign requests for finding teabags or how to stem the flow of supermarket brochures filling their letterboxes. On a good day, the responses were low and hard-hitting, reminding me of Wild West movies with people shooting from the hip, just for kicks. Its saving grace was the occasional pearls of wisdom that interspersed the rugged behaviour. During this particular online sojourn I was on the hunt for one of these pearls. Not that I was supposed to be on Facebook, I was supposed to be finding a new language school and doing my Danish homework, which lay unopened on the overflowing bookcase next to my desk. The boredom of both tasks sent me procrastinating into the expat rambling rabbit hole in which I was now embroiled.

"Urgh," I exhaled as I stood up, trying to distance myself from the online rants and ramblings. *Why do I do that?* An hour had passed since I sat down. An hour I was never getting back. Closing my computer, I snapped out of my zombie state created by the mindless scrolling and headed off in search of the source of the monotone reverberations that had interrupted my lethargy. *A little break will do me good,* I thought.

Walking into the kitchen, the two other members of the household were huddled over the large stainless-steel mixing bowl, hypnotically watching the Danish medley of rye, seeds and grains transform into a dense brown mixture. The kitchen was more his domain than mine, not that I'd fought that hard for ownership of it. He, together with the small selection of other Danish men I'd so far been introduced to, were all excellent in the kitchen. They all seemed very at home in the cooking department. Whereas trying to make anything with ingredients whose label I couldn't read gave me a headache.

"That time of the week is it?" I asked, referencing The Dane's weekly ritual of making *rugbrød* (rye bread), a dark brown rye loaf, whose density and weight was similar to a brick. Not that I could pronounce it. The ongoing impossible-ness of the 'o' with a slash had made me briefly consider converting to a gluten-free diet in the hope I could avoid saying it altogether. But I quickly gave up on the idea as I realised rugbrød was king in Vikingland and there was no escape. It was a compulsory item in Danish shopping trollies. The locals loved the stuff, which literally had the ability to untether your bowels. Fridges and breadboxes throughout the country were full of it. Its dominance was so great, it was hard to imagine the government weren't issuing loaves of the stuff to every newborn in the country. Dense dark bread was in their DNA and, keeping them regular.

Lunch in Denmark is as topless as a convertible car on a sunny day. Rugbrød should be eaten with toppings, not fillings. Fillings imply a second slice should be added which is not how it is done in Denmark. One slice only, on the bottom. Keep it topless.

"What's that?" I asked, pointing at the small plastic bottle The Dane was squirting into the bowl.

"Brown colouring," he replied, without lifting his eyes from the bowl, oblivious to the mini-convulsions I was having while my mouth hung open. What was or wasn't brown bread had been a hot topic between us, with him insisting only his heavy, bowel-cleansing rye speciality was fit to be called brown bread. My pale multigrain toast bread was not brown enough by Danish standards.

A child in New Zealand eating a multigrain sandwich for lunch would be a nutritional hero. In Denmark, they'll be noted by some for eating unhealthy white bread with a swirl of nutritional stigma hovering over them like a dirty halo.

"But is it really brown bread if you have to put brown colouring in it?" I asked.

"You don't have to put it in," he clarified. "It just makes it look nicer." *What a load of crap*, I harshly concluded, unconvinced with the logic. Continuing to pour the wet rye mixture into the red silicone loaf moulds, he was oblivious to my shock.

"Hold on," I said gathering my thoughts. "For the last seven years you've fed me the line that rugbrød, the holy grail of Danish madkasser [lunchboxes] was THE definition of brown bread. Now you're telling me the colour comes out of a bottle?" I asked, unable to hold back my balking tones.

"It's still got more grains than you'll ever find in a loaf of multigrain," he replied, tucking his secret colouring weapon back into the pantry.

I'd often wondered what that bottle was for, but had never thought to ask. He was a very talented baker, but this explanation, I decided, was a bit bollocks.

"You know Denmark's got its own Whole Grain Partnership? Did you know that?" He proudly played his trump card from his fountain of random Danish facts.

Of course I didn't know that. "They do?" I replied, trying my best to be productive in the conversation.

"And they get it from rugbrød, not white bread," he concluded as he smoothed the wet mixture into the bread moulds.

The Danish Whole Grain Partnership (*Fuldkornspartnerskabet*) encourages Danes to eat more whole grains in order to improve public health. The Danes eat an average 82g of whole grain per day and 50% of the Danish population now eat the recommended amount of 75g whole grain per day. Brown bread is in their blood.

Scientific facts aside, I wasn't ready to let this go just yet. *If there was ever a moment to win this brown bread debate, it's now,* I thought. Taking a seat at the dining room table, I began strategising how best to present my case. Plopping **BBB** on to the floor, the breadmaker of the household threw a tea towel over the bread before placing it in the sunlight streaming through the kitchen windows. *Is a Dane still a Dane without rugbrød?* I wondered. My relationship with the stuff was in its infancy and I was yet to understand its popularity with the masses.

Staring at the incriminating bottle of brown food colouring on the open pantry shelf, I wondered what other dark Danish secrets there were to discover as BBB bum-shuffled her way over to me, none the wiser to the hysteria I was whipping up.

"Is this also shared in your daily Danish memo?" I asked, referencing the uncanny ability of the nation to be talking about the same thing on the same day. This was a phenomenon I'd decided had to be the result of everyone receiving a memo with a list of approved topics to discuss on any said day. A memo that was never shared with me.

"What?" came the distracted reply from The Dane with a rightfully injected hint of annoyance.

"To add brown food colouring to your 'brown' bread," I asked doing my best 12-year-old tattletale voice as I stressed the word 'brown'.

"Yeah, sure," he replied, indicating my fun with this Great Brown Bread Debate was over, for today at least.

"Shall we go pick the berries, as soon as this comes out?" he asked, setting the timer on the oven.

I'd forgotten about the blackberry (*brombær*) agreement. They grew wild like weeds, and we'd spied a monster row of bushes a few weeks earlier and agreed to come back to try our luck foraging once they'd ripened. I made some mental notes so we could finish the rugbrød brown bread debate later.

Vikings of all sizes are encouraged to be outdoors, find edible food in nature and use what the land provides them with in season. Something they embrace and do often.

Forbidden Fruit

Surely that monster crop has gotta be in no man's land? I thought. We were standing on the single-lane country road with BBB in her pram. In front of us, a bonanza crop of forgotten blackberries lay before us, surrounded by a smattering of freshly ploughed fields. Eager to get started, BBB was chucking overboard the empty yoghurt containers I'd stashed in her pram to collect our haul in. Behind us, The Dane scanned the horizon in search of someone to ask permission from so we could begin picking what looked like to me an abandoned crop.

"Do we really need to find someone?" I asked The Dane. "They're ages away," I said pointing towards the farmhouse in the distance, which he was intent on approaching. "They can't even see them from their place." Exploding with growth, I doubted the prickly bushes had ever been on the receiving end of any horticultural loving. Their entire purpose seemed to be just dividing two properties. *No one's going to miss a few,* I thought.

"Yes," the Dane confirmed as he strode towards the century-old thatched roofed farm buildings in the distance. Even with the overgrown vegetation threatening to take over the property, it was obvious the buildings also needed some attention. Waiting on the road while he followed the gravel path towards the run-down farmhouse, I mused that the farmers would have been lucky to even see out their windows, let alone see what we were doing 500m down the road. They wouldn't have even known we were there. Re-emerging after a few minutes, The Dane traversed his way back along the overgrown path giving me a nod. "We can pick them. But only what we can reach from the road." The second part of his harvest briefing floated over me.

Retracing our steps, we headed back along the road to the forgotten and grossly out-of-control blackberries. *What we could reach from the road is only the tip of the iceberg,* I enthusiastically thought, picturing the jars of jam I'd make later. Beyond the first row of bushes I could see even more bushes drowning in fruit. Towering wildly above me, at least half the fruit was impossible to reach from the ground. We parked BBB in a shady spot and got to work.

"I don't think they've pruned the bushes in a while," I said detangling my t-shirt that had become impaled in a web of thorns. Wrestling with my shirt, my gaze landed on an enormous spread of blackberries just out of my non-Viking arms' reach from the road. Freeing myself from the bush, the forbidden fruit lured me forward and I took a handful of steps off the road to reach for them. Concentrating on not impaling myself again, I became lost in my quest for plucking the biggest berries that I could lay my hands on. It didn't matter they were all destined for the jam pot and would soon be indistinguishable pulp.

"Hey!"

Pivoting on my toes, I swung around to find a Viking Farmer-type striding at a good clip across the field. A long-forgotten memory of a charging rhino I saw on safari in Zambia jumped back into my head. His yelling intensified with every stride. Even though I hadn't reached Danish proficiency yet, the swiftness of his strides made it obvious I was in trouble.

"Incoming…" I mumbled as innocently as I could to The Dane as the pre-harvest briefing began ringing in my ears and my stomach filled with a bucketful of mortification. Scampering the few metres back up to the road, I hid behind my protector, in the exact fashion that I imagined BBB would do in a few years when she was trying to avoid something unpleasant.

"What were you doing?" he hissed at me with remarkable restraint given the circumstances, as he clocked the raging Farmer approaching. I acted dumb, both from an intellectual and verbal point of view, which seemed the smartest choice for the present moment. My rudimentary Danish was unlikely to be any help at talking my way out of this social faux pas. Hiding behind The Dane, I left it to him to explain the cultural misunderstanding regarding the roadside harvest foraging rules.

Five minutes later, the Farmer retreated across his field, back to his camouflaged farm barns. I gave it a few more minutes before I stepped out of The Dane's shadow, dreading the conversation to come.

"What were you doing over there?" he asked, waving halfway along the overgrown hedge. "They told us to only pick what we could reach from the road."

"It was just a couple of steps off the road," I replied more as a question than a statement, as I looked back at the scene of the incident.

"You were 20 metres down the fence line," The Dane corrected, ushering me back to the safe zone of the road.

Looking along the monster crop, he was annoyingly right.

"But there's no way anyone could ever use all of those berries. I would've happily brought back a jar of jam as a thank you," I argued.

"You didn't follow the rule," The Dane replied.

A loud sigh escaped my mouth. My casual creative interpretation of the rules was at odds with the locals and I realised I felt culturally chastised. Danes were great rule-followers. My previously proper-ish ways had become perfectly improper.

Dear ground, please open and swallow me whole.

In Denmark, the rules are the rules, which is why you'll see someone waiting for the green cross light at 7am on a Sunday morning when the nearest car is 2km away. Creative interpretation of the rules is never expected and is why one should never reach for the forbidden fruit.

Confrontations

Later that evening, after putting **BBB** to bed, we escaped to the balcony while the first batch of blackberry jam boiled on the induction stove. Every window and door in the apartment was open in the vague hope a whiff of a cool breeze would find its way into our brick inferno. I poured myself a large glass of New Zealand Sauvignon Blanc, its contents sloshing perilously close to the top of the glass.

"Thirsty?" The Dane asked, noticing my haste to down the fermented grape juice.

I opened my mouth to answer but was interrupted by the unmistakable sound of drumsticks clicking together. The noise came from the other side of the trees that separated our apartment from the row of houses behind it. The clacking sounded urgent. Seconds later live music began to blare, rattling my jam jars warming in the oven.

"What the feck?" I uttered, staring at The Dane for an explanation on the acoustic attack.

"I guess the birthday party is still going on?" he replied. We'd heard some noise at lunchtime before we went out, but that was eight hours earlier. *Surely it can't be the same one?* I thought, shocked by the stamina of partying Vikings as a festival of amplified music was unleashed from beyond our communal hedge. A nameless neighbour began banging pots on her balcony while shouting at them to shut up.

"Is that the normal approach for confronting neighbours?" I asked The Dane. "Why doesn't she just go over and talk to them instead of doing, whatever that is, on her balcony. They're not going to hear that."

"That's true," The Dane agreed. "Why don't you go and tell them to turn it down instead?"

Confrontation (big or small) is not a trait routinely found in Denmark. Some commentators of Denmark will sell this as an endearing feature and tell a story about how Danes prefer to continue talking until they find some common ground. In reality, what it means is, if you're an idiot, you can expect to get away with it as very few will rise to tell you to knock it on the head.

Bonus insight: When hosting a party in Denmark it's common (if not expected) to send a note to your neighbours to warn them in advance.

He was right, of course, I thought, as I desperately wracked my brain for an excuse why I shouldn't go over.

"How do I tell them in Danish?" I asked.

"Just tell them in English. They're young. They'll understand," he replied as I fought to keep my monolingual fears under control. Unlike my Danish neighbours, when equipped with the right language I did confrontation well, but here in Vikingland it was difficult to replicate it. I was being sent to the frontline to sort out the neighbourhood disturbance with only one language in my verbal arsenal. I tried to ignore the waves of vulnerability that flooded my head.

"Sure," I replied with all the false bravado that half a bottle of New Zealand Sauvignon Blanc offered.

Monolingual butterflies started twirling in my stomach as I made my way along the street to the suburban surprise rock fest. *Please let them be okay about speaking English,* I prayed as I walked up the gravel driveway. A half-child-half-man-looking Viking greeted me halfway, his tuxedo signalling he had power of some kind.

"I'm sorry," I started, unsure why I was apologising to him. "But your music is too loud."

"It's my birthday!" he responded in perfect English with all the excitement of a five-year-old.

"How old?" I asked, his enthusiasm infectious and filling me with curiosity.

"Twenty!" he smiled back at me.

Twenty? Just twenty and you've got a live band playing in your backyard? I thought, puzzled by the calibre of the party for just a 20th, wondering where I went wrong as I remembered the Gorilla Gram my parents had arranged for my 21st. Before I knew it, my mouth opened in an uncontrollable middle-aged lady moment.

"Oh! You're so young," I flapped in genuine shock, as I stared at his enthusiastic body language, yet to be chipped away at.

"Huh? Um, okay we'll turn it down then," he replied, unsure what else to say before nervously walking backwards down the garden path away from me.

The DNA of a Dane

A week later, sitting apprehensively in my new Danish language class, I let the distraction of the swaying venetian blinds mesmerise me. A steady breeze entered from the windows wide open behind them. Afternoon sun flooded the room, rendering the whiteboard useless, as an eclectic mash of street noises wafted their way up to our fourth floor classroom from the *Nordvest* streets below. An infusing mix of Middle Eastern grocery shops, shawarma joints and bakeries lined the streets.

Authoritarian Agnes had been replaced by Anna, another long-legged local, to whom I was trying to give my full attention. I managed to drag my awareness back from life outside the window just in time as she set our next task.

"What do you think are the most important Danish values?" Anna asked as she split us into three groups to dissect the inner workings of Danes – something we spent an uncomfortable amount of time discussing in class.

The topic immediately sent my mind racing back to the previous weekend's Blackberry Crimes. My cheeks began to blush spontaneously, mortification still fresh in my mind. *Well, at least I've learnt that following the rules is important,* I told myself.

Discussing Danish values, along with whether we enjoyed living in Denmark, was becoming a regular feature in class, frequently causing my eyes to roll into the back of my head. I wanted to learn how to hold a conversation with my daughter's friends in Danish that wouldn't induce her in future years to roll her eyes at me. Gaining a vocabulary to debate Danish values wasn't one I imagined I'd have much need for. *Unless I was to go foraging for blackberries again, of course,* I thought. The constant analysis of Danish DNA made it feel like I'd enrolled in Danish Grooming School, rather than a language school. It had me wondering if the government was making the most of Dane-ifying as many of us foreigners as possible while they had their chance. I pondered if, after I'd mastered the language, I'd actually be considered Danish. *Unlikely,* I thought, answering my own question. I'd probably have to develop an incurable need to eat herrings on rugbrød first. Something I didn't see happening anytime soon.

"*Hvad er det vigtigste for dig?*" the teacher asked, pouncing on me for my opinion, startling me like a rabbit caught in the headlights. *At least she didn't slam my book shut,* I thought. *This is progress.*

Hovering over her electronic whiteboard, Anna waited for me to tell her what I thought. Trying to invent an answer that matched my Danish vocabulary, I began marvelling at how her pencil long legs and arms enabled her to reach all four corners of the board with ease. *That top third of the board wouldn't be seeing much action if I was the teacher,* I unnecessarily considered as I reflected on my Hobbit-esque stature, which had the locals regularly towering over me.

"*Frisind, frihed or tillid?*" (Liberty, freedom or trust?) she asked again, prompting me from my procrastinating state.

Not ready to share the blackberry incident just yet, I instead began trawling my memory banks for another example. *How about the liberal and free application of the brown food colouring in rye bread?* I thought as I wondered whether I had the vocabulary to flesh that thought into a coherent sentence. Giving up on that idea I replied that I thought trust was very important: "*Jeg tror, at tillid er meget vigtigt.*" I attempted to suck my tongue to the bottom of my mouth to push the double 'l' and soft 'd' from my vocal cords that had not previously been required to bend in such a manner. *Well, that's a bitch of a word,* I noted.

Unperturbed with my less-than-perfect pronunciation, eager anticipation spread across her encouraging face. She seemed a lot more excited than I was to be discussing the topic.

"*Hvorfor?*" came her predictable, one-word response, enquiring why I believed that to be true, as she tried to pry more Danish from my lips.

In 2016 the Danish government released a list of 10 important values (as voted for by the public) that have shaped Danish society. These were collected via a survey called the *Danmarkskanon (Denmark Canon).* Insert drumroll. The 10 most important values were:

The Christian heritage
The Danish language
Associations and voluntary work
Liberality/tolerance
Hygge
Gender equality
Equality for the law
Freedom
Trust
Welfare Society

Using my miniscule Danish vocabulary, I eventually cobbled some nouns and adjectives together.

"Pastries and bicycles are very important in Denmark. Therefore, so is trust."

Undeniably, it was a rubbish sentence with Anna's face quickly confirming she thought the same.

"What do you mean," she probed further, doing her best to encourage me.

A fair question, I thought because I had no clue what I meant by it either.

'Trust' was a word touted and flouted in Vikingland almost as much as 'hygge', the Danish concept of all things cosy, candles and cake-ish that the rest of the world had grown an obsession to. *Surely, I can think of something more to say?* I asked myself.

Danes grew up bathed in the concept of trust. Something I'd witnessed by just looking out our apartment window at our neighbours putting their children outside to sleep in their prams (albeit with a baby monitor). Or by the farmers who left bundles of their produce by their farm gates knowing people would pay for what they took. Restaurants and cafés in Copenhagen left tables and chairs outside overnight, safe in the knowledge they'd still be there the next day. These were daily reminders of how much trust was taken for granted in Vikingland.

None of these thoughts, of course, could I translate into Danish. The restraints on my vocal cords gave me no ability to connect them to the random sentence I'd just unleashed, and which was still reverberating around the classroom making no sense. My fellow students cocked their heads up from their notebooks and smartphones in the hope my body language might have given them a clue.

"Last weekend I picked blackberries, but I didn't follow the rules and the farmer was angry."

"*Hvorfor?*" she asked, as I sensed a mild dash of judgment and shock towards my scandalous behaviour.

"Because he trusted me to follow the rules," I unnecessarily capitulated. My limited vocabulary caused an unplanned confession.

"I understand," Anna began, the attempt to hide her disappointment failing as she realised it was a true story. "But what does that have to do with bikes and pastries?"

"Nothing," I said, shrugging my shoulders in the hope it was now one of my fellow classmate's turn to make an arse of themselves in Danish. Conversations often went like that in class, as we attempted to string opinions together from our tiny vocabularies.

On cue, Catherine, the American who always sat in the front row with her jumbo-sized drink bottle, interrupted with her own awkward Danish contribution. Thankful that the attention was now thrust in her direction, I grabbed my phone and Googled 'Danish Values' in the hope it would help me understand what the DNA of a Dane was.

Nine, Daily Life With a Dane

Børnehave Fluency

It was week three of BBB's Danish education, a hub of one-to-six-year-olds hanging out en masse and wearing dazzlingly bright mini hi-viz vests when waddling in public. It was a sight that sent me running for my camera with unreasonable delight every time.

During the rare conversations I'd had with other parents before she started, they'd told me if mini-Vikings weren't at *vuggestue* (nursery) when they turned one, then you'd be in the minority. *Barsel* (parental leave) was for a year (ish), and after that their offspring would start vuggestue. *Barsel* was a defined period with clear expectations. This formula allowed the Vikingland parents to return to work easily after procreating to make the most of their government-funded education (master's degrees in most cases) in the real world. It wasn't about offloading their kids for the day; it was about best utilising tax contributions from over the years. Not that any of that logic quietened my guilt as I dropped BBB off every morning and returned to our empty apartment. *I was yet to crack the Danish job market, so why did we need childcare?* I'd wondered.

Oblivious to my quandary, BBB was having a great time at vuggestue, her social life flourishing while I languished in a lonely space and tried to find my rhythm. Settling into the new routine was tough. My days continued to be filled with the soul-squashing activities of completing my Danish homework and searching for a job in a foreign market in which I was just another foreigner. Both activities brought me as much joy as poking toothpicks in my eyeballs. *Was I living my best life in Denmark? Would I ever?* It felt like 'Keri from New Zealand' had been packed up like a summer wardrobe and was now laying forgotten somewhere under the bed.

Dismounting from my bike, I didn't need to check my reflection in the nursery's front doors to know I looked like a woman woefully out of her league in the fight against the Danish weather gods.

Even with my protective Danish outerwear, a very on-trend *regnjakke* (rain jacket), I'd managed to fail miserably at cycling the pathetically short 700m to BBB's *vuggestue*. My jeans clung heavily to my thighs where my 3/4 rain jacket stopped. My freshly washed and straightened hair was now a sodden mess, giving me a greater understanding for the Danish popularity of tying up long hair in messy topknots. *God only knows how those Danes manage to do it,* I wondered, looking at the other parents who all looked effortlessly presentable and dry as they dropped off their children.

Parking my bike, water squelched out from my inadequately waterproofed Skechers. Perched behind me, BBB was still strapped in her cycle seat. Clinging on like a monkey in a tropical storm, she hadn't fared much better than me, even her small amount of hair was now plastered in wet clumps across her face.

"Well, at least your gumboots match your jacket," I said, admiring one of the rare occasions I'd successfully colour co-ordinated an outfit. *That's worthy of bonus parenting points.*

Childcare for 0–5 year olds in Denmark is impressively subsidised by the government. In Copenhagen, sending a 5 year-old to *børnehave* will cost you around 2,500 DKK per month including lunch.

Bonus insight: *Børnehave* is the name given to the institutions 3-5 year-olds attend, whereas *vuggestue* is the name of the institution for 0-3 year-olds.

Shaking the excess water from my helmet before entering the building, BBB and I began an awkward dance of removing our rain clothes. Pint-sized wooden lockers lined the cloakroom walls with a small cupboard at the top and a mini-sized bench seat at the bottom. Each locker sported the child's name together with the sensible back-up system of an animal picture in case they didn't recognise their name yet. BBB was a goldfish, which was quite apt for our arrival today. I grabbed a pair of blue shoe covers from the communal box inside the front door, pulling them over my now sodden Skechers.

Stretching along the side of the building was a gaggle of stationary prams – each the size of a small tractor with industrial-strength, black weathered canvas coverings. This was where BBB and her fellow mini-Vikings took their naps. The outdoor dormitory was permanently parked under a small awning, shielding the cherubs from the worst of the weather as they slept. My non-Scandinavian

DNA still found the sleeping arrangement a bit of an unnecessary spectacle. Something non-Danes felt drawn to taking photos when they got the chance, myself included. 'Fresh air helps them sleep, it's good for them' and 'don't worry, we'll bring them in if it reaches minus 10 degrees' were among the words of wisdom and reassurance shared with me when we signed up. The realisation that my daughter would be sleeping outside in sun, snow and sleet had left me non-plussed. She, however, had inherited her father's heartiness for the situation.

Looking down, I saw that water was pooling in my compulsory blue shoe covers and seeped and squelched out as I walked. I should have just taken them off. We had the choice of taking off our shoes when entering the building or wearing the shoe covers. For fear of standing barefoot on a half-eaten piece of broccoli, I'd always chosen the latter, but was beginning to see merit in the alternative.

"Alright, let's get you out of this before my feet drown," I told BBB, stripping off her bright purple rain jacket and pants and hanging them in her locker. I carefully placed her matching gumboots underneath, but slightly to the left of the dripping rain gear. Fishing around at the bottom of the locker, with my bum stuck antisocially in the air, I eventually found BBB's impossibly small *hjemmesko* (indoor shoes) and changed her into them.

Holding a marginally less damp BBB on my hip, with her *madpakke* (packed lunch) in my other hand, we headed towards the classroom. I caught my reflection in the wall of circus mirrors that lined the corridor to entertain the mini-Vikings. My short, chubby, damp smurf-like appearance seemed to be magnified tenfold. It wasn't my best look, striking for all the wrong reasons. *A picture only a mother could love,* I mused. Ignoring my reflection, I swung open the childproof gate into the classroom and stepped into the den.

In the far corner the popular madpakke table was a hive of toddler food antics as they attacked their snack boxes. I'd decided it was a 'hygge in training' table equipping the mini-Vikings with the survival skills they'd need in later life: to sit around a dining room table for five hours at Danish parties.

Attracted like bees to a honeypot, half the mini-Vikings were waiting for a sloppy plateful of warm porridge topped with a generous scoop of sugar while the other half ripped into their own lunchboxes from home. Annette, the kitchen lady, with her full-length navy and white stripped apron that was already smeared with the day's offerings, was at the helm feeding breakfast to those who wanted it.

In three short weeks the madpakke table had become both mine and BBB's highlight of the day. BBB was attracted by the sugary porridge, while the realisation I could actually understand what the older kids were saying gave me a small amount of renewed enthusiasm for learning Danish. It seemed that after nearly a year in Denmark I had possibly reached kindergarten fluency as I navigated my way through several mini-Viking natterings. I might not always have understood every word they said, but was on my way.

"*Kan du hjælpe med at åbne min salami*," Emil asked, waving a pre-packaged mini salami stick in my face, something he did every day in the hope that I would open it for him. I thought it was quite decent of him to include me like that considering I'd yet to work out how to pronounce his name.

"*Selvfølgelig*," (of course) I responded using one of the handful of Danish words I'd now mastered.

Emil loved a good yarn, telling me long stories of presumably his weekend antics, not bothered with my lack of Danish vocabulary nor my inability to swallow my d's. Unlike his elders, he wasn't even fussed with the acoustic disaster that erupted from my mouth when I tried to pronounce the Danish word for bread (*brød*). That little 'o' with the line slashing through it was forever my enemy.

The top three phrases for making small talk with small people in Danish are: 1. *Hvad laver du?* (What are you doing?); 2. *Det er ikke så godt* (That's not so good.); and 3. *Er det rigtigt?* (Is that right?). Give it a whirl, you'll see what I mean.

Ripping out the rest of the contents from his madpakke, Emil began excitedly displaying his line-up of edible goods, while BBB began experimenting, stirring her porridge until the slop started projecting across the table. Not that either of them was hungry. I could guarantee Emil, like BBB, would have just had breakfast at home. The madpakke frenzy each morning was more about snack eating entertainment, not essential sustenance.

Cucumber sticks, grapes and a plastic-looking cheese stick came flying in my direction in quick succession as Emil waited for my votes of approval.

Opening the salami stick, I did my best to be impressed with the edible ensemble displayed in front of me as he launched into another conversation before I could escape.

"*Er det rigtigt?*" I answered, to whatever it was coming from his mouth. The verbal diarrhoea bore down on me at a rate of knots and had me scrambling to follow. Emil had just turned four and I suspected was soon to cotton on to my language limitations.

Viggo's mother (which seemed to be the naming system for refer-ring to other parents when you had no idea what their name was) whose hair was neither wet nor sticking to her head in a tangled mess like mine, watched our exchange from the other end of the table. Her head cocked to the side, her eyebrows becoming tangled in what looked like discomfort, as Emil continued repeating the undistinguishable phrase to me. I smiled broadly in return, confidentially letting her know it was okay, I wasn't bothered.

Waving goodbye to BBB, who was happy as a pig in mud playing with the warm bowl of oat slop in front of her, I returned to the cloakroom to put my rain gear back on and head out into the weather again. Dropping my soggy shoe protectors in the reusable bin for the next parent to borrow, Viggo's mother caught up with me.

"Did you understand what Emil was saying?" she asked, sounding strangely concerned. Relieved of the opportunity of full disclosure I took the opportunity to confess.

"Actually, I'm not sure. Was it something about his lunchbox?" I replied, beginning to doubt myself as Viggo's mother's expression remained neutral, suggesting that hadn't been what he was saying to me. "Why, what was he telling me?" I asked.

"Emil was calling you a farting shit."

Maybe I hadn't quite reached kindergarten fluency, I realised as my gut filled with a mix of embarrassment and disappointment.

"He did?"

"Yeah, he probably picked it up from some of the older kids and was just trying it out," she politely offered.

Smiling weakly, I thanked her for the translation before heading to my bike and the safety of our empty apartment to complete the rest of my soul-squashing tasks for the day.

Slut (finish) and *fart* (speed), two Danish words guaranteed to make a native English speaker giggle like a kid. And 'shit'? That'll be *lort* as in a farting *lort*.

The Family Calendar

Startling me, The Dane walked through the front door unannounced. I glanced at the clock hanging on the kitchen wall.

2pm

"Did you get fired?" I asked, skipping the expected standard hello greeting. I'd become accustomed to The Dane arriving home at 3pm, but this unexpected arrival was entering a new zone. I'd only just had lunch.

"No, it's Friday," he replied in a tone suggesting it was his complete, full and final answer.

Before his unexpected appearance, I'd been trying to decipher our family wall calendar while also congratulating myself on making it to the end of the week having only been called a 'farting shit' once. The wall calendar didn't look like a calendar to me. It was more like a glorified spreadsheet with bonus folklore pictures. Its vertical format had an impossibly small font that challenged my orientation of the weekend ahead, as I attempted to make sense of the Danish week numbering system. I took the opportunity to double check what day of the week it was, as if that might give me a clue as to why The Dane was home so early.

Friday.

Looking out the window, there was a heavier than normal stream of traffic and bicycles marching like ants past our apartment. *They clearly think it's Friday too,* I thought. It was as if the entire nation had all received the same instruction to up sticks from their desks and begin the weekend promptly at 2pm.

"And I'd finished my work for the week," The Dane added.

Makes sense, I silently agreed, marvelling at the efficiency of both executing a 37-hour week, the norm in Denmark, and his ability to switch into weekend mode mid-afternoon on a Friday while my weekly orbit radar lagged behind. I hadn't even had my Friday afternoon smoko yet.

"What do we have on this weekend?" he asked, noticing my desperate stares at the calendar.

"Something at Lars and Lene's?" I replied, while still not sure if I was looking at the right day. "Is it Lars Larsen?" I asked as an excuse to roll the rhythmical double-banger name off my tongue for fun as an entirely inappropriate schoolgirl smirk spread across my face.

"Yes, Lars Larsen and Lene's," The Dane confirmed, deciding to ignore the immature amusement in my voice. No one ever said Lene's surname, it didn't roll off the tongue as well.

My eyebrows started dancing in delight at the sound of the double Danish name. This prolific naming trend was systemic to the Viking world and filled me with much amusement every time I came across it. Walking the streets with BBB, I delighted in reading the names on all the letterboxes, hoping to stumble across one of the many Henrik Henriksens, Jens Jensens, Anders Andersens or Jesper Jespersens who were generously scattered throughout the neighbourhood. Danish Double Banger Bingo was the name I'd given the game. Having one within our own social network felt a bit like hitting the jackpot, not that I told anyone that.

"What time?" I asked, giving up on trying to decode any further details on the calendar.

"3pm."

I'd been to enough 'coffees' in Denmark to know this wasn't going to be a casual pop-in kind of affair, and if I wanted to add any other activity into our day I'd need to be creative. Otherwise it would be a full-day event.

"Great. There's a *loppemarked* (secondhand market) on the way, can we leave a bit earlier and check it out first?" I suggested, more as a statement than a question.

"Uh huh," came the non-committal reply from the Viking with an allergy to nick-nacks. A loppemarked was his worst nightmare.

"Don't you need to go and pick up BBB?" I reminded him, jolting him back to the present moment as I glanced over at the kitchen clock. At 3pm he was going to be one of the last parents to pick up.

"Uh huh," he repeated, grabbing his cycle helmet and disappearing out the door again to retrieve BBB like a man who'd dodged a bullet, a welcome escape from further loppemarked discussions.

Treasure on the Sidewalk

Loading BBB's pram the next day with five spare nappies, three changes of clothes, a water bottle, baby wipes, a change mat, blanket and a plastic phone with animal ringtones, we set off at a good trot for the 30-minute walk to Lars Larsen and Lene's.

"Why so much stuff?" asked The Dane.

"This coffee is going to take at least three hours, I guarantee you," I replied. If I'd learnt one thing about the social habits of Danes in my first months living in Denmark, it was that there's no such thing as a 'quick cuppa'. An invite for coffee was hygge time and not to be rushed.

Turning the corner, I stopped abruptly; I was in heaven. I had found the loppemarked.

Before us lay rows of impeccably well-organised stands lining both sides of the streets – the stallholders lived in the apartment buildings behind them. Each stand was covered with a treasure trove of used goods.

"Wow!" I squealed.

The Dane remained silent, likely in horror as he calculated how this would impact on our coffee date.

Covering the tables were boxes of toys, books, clothes, DVDs, crockery and IKEA nick-nacks (my favourite kind). The display of the items was on par with a high-street shop with hangers, labels and an impressive ordering of sizes. Some racks were even ordered by colour. A throng of fellow bargain hunters swooped along the street, inspecting the goods. It was a bit like a Kiwi garage sale, but a hundred times classier.

Looking along the street, I began surveying where I should explore in hope of some quick toys and clothes bargains for BBB.

"We've still got time for a quick look, don't we?" I asked.

"Not really. We need to be there at three," The Dane replied, anxiously looking at his watch to calculate our remaining walk time. From previous social engagements I knew arriving exactly on time was important, and you had to make it a priority to arrive bang on the time you were invited for.

"It's two twenty now, there's time." I smiled in what I hoped was a convincing fashion. "It's only another ten minutes from here," I added, not knowing where I'd got the crude guestimation from. Parking BBB's pram next to her father I began foraging through a box of children's books. *Well at least this should be less stressful than foraging for blackberries,* I thought. The feelings of mortification flooded back as I remembered the 'incident' that had sent me scuttling behind The Dane like a five-year-old.

Paying for the books, I looked up to see The Dane's head bobbing away from me through the crowd that was continuing to build. This market must be a good one if it attracted all these people. Heading off to catch The Dane, I scanned the remaining stands as I made my way towards him. Stopping at another stand I did a quick rummage of the raingear and shoes on offer. Snatching up a pair of black Nike sneakers and a set of *regnbukser* (rain trousers), I eventually caught up to The

Dane the end of the street. Like a pro, he'd managed to avoid walking with me for the entire length of the market, ensuring I surveyed the stalls in record time while jogging to catch up with him. As the crowd parted, the rest of his body became visible at last. Following the line of his arms I automatically looked downward for the pram with **BBB** inside where I could stow my loppemarked treasures away. Alarmingly there was nothing attached to the end of his arms, just hands – two, rather ordinary Viking hands.

"Where's our daughter?'

"You had her," he replied.

"I parked her next to you!" I shot back, while realising I hadn't given an explicit supervisory message to him.

Turning simultaneously on our heels, like a pair of well-oiled synchronised swimmers, we sprinted back up the street fighting against the tide of pedestrians crossing in all directions in search of our misplaced child.

"Fark!" I exclaimed, not exhaling until we reached the top of the street.

Like a lighthouse tower, I pivoted in search of the stand with the impeccably displayed goods and clothes hanging by size and colour with individual price tags, where we'd started our bargain hunting, and where I'd parked our child out of the way.

"There!" I yelled as I pointed towards the path behind the table, where I'd left her under the supervision of The Dane. Since then a swarm of adjacent prams, both flat-bed and the sit-up variety, had appeared. Ours was no longer visible. The Dane, who was looking more like a Golden Retriever, pushed past me and trotted down the path in search of our accidentally abandoned one. He made a sweeping search of the row of parked mini-Viking wagons.

"Here she is!" The Dane trumpeted proudly, trotting back up the cobblestone path (or cobble-wobblers as I'd taken to calling them) with BBB still asleep in her pram.

"Thank goodness we found her!" he exclaimed with a rare display of emotion.

BBB was oblivious to her temporary parental abandonment and, if we were lucky, would never become aware of this parental lapse.

I wondered how long an unattended baby in a pram could go before becoming a point of concern in a country where most babies slept outside. Deciding it wasn't worth dwelling on for too long, I motioned back along the street, towards Lars Larsen and Lene's.

"Shall we?"

Loppemarked season in Denmark is strongest in spring and autumn. These are secondhand markets where you can find anything and everything; a goldmine of excitement for a bargain hunter to explore. Anyone can organise their own Loppemarked, but it's also very common for neighbours to collectively organise a bigger Loppemarked that takes over their street.

The Three-hour Coffee

Quickening his pace, The Dane hurriedly knocked on Lene and Lars Larsen's front door at precisely 3:02pm. We were two minutes late and The Dane's disappointment was visible: his shoulders slumped.

"At least we didn't have to hover by the doorbell waiting for the clock to strike three before we could ring the bell, right?" I suggested in hope it'd lighten the mood, sensing The Dane was yet to forgive me for temporarily misplacing our child.

"*Hej*! Welcome. Come inside," Lene greeted us with a mix of handshaking and hugs.

We stepped inside the classic shoe and jacket depository room I'd come to expect in Vikingland, which was lined with coats and boots for every season and possible weather combination, and where Lene continued to greet us warmly. Taking The Dane's lead, I kicked off my shoes while balancing **BBB** on my hip, a little smugly, knowing we'd managed not to lose her in the remainder of our walk to their house. We followed behind Lene to the heart of their home, the dining room table. The Dane and his family spent hours sitting around theirs – I likened it to the love Kiwis have for their sofa, although with more class and manners. The sofa was where I was more accustomed to sitting for hours.

Candles and Royal Copenhagen coffee cups, together with some sort of woodland arrangement, lay on the table. Like something from the Danish *Home and Garden* magazine (if there was such a thing); it looked like a Pinterest board for hygge.

"Oh, sorry. I haven't got the napkins out yet," Lene apologised before we'd even sat down. Sensing this must have been a type of Danish social crime, I watched her hurriedly open a small drawer in the pale oak wall cabinet behind us. An array of paper napkins lay exposed, the drawer bulging with napkins of every colour and size.

"Wow," I said for the second time that day. "Is that your napkin drawer?" I asked, unable to play it cool with the impressive assortment.

"Err. I guess you could call it that?" Lene replied, her brow slightly twisted in what I recognised as either she hadn't understood my accent, or my sense of humour. It was a look I received fairly often. As Lene tried to unscramble her brow, Lars Larsen popped out from the kitchen.

"*Hej*! Welcome!" Lars offered as he walked towards us with his hand outstretched for the compulsory handshake.

"*Hej*, Lars," I said, biting my tongue to stop me from adding his surname.

"Sit, sit," he instructed as he placed two cylindrical Rosendahl thermal coffee pots on the table in front of us. Our supplies for the next three hours.

Sitting down, Lene added a selection of small bowls of nuts and grapes to the table. The Dane switched into Danish while I switched into smiling dummy mode, thankful for BBB to busy myself with. I was looking forward to her being my translator in a few years.

Reaching for the coffee pot, I nervously pressed and twisted anything that would move on it. Every one of these damn things had a different system to pour them. Eventually, with a loud pop, I managed to serve myself a cup and reached for the tiny jug of milk on the table. It looked more ornamental than functional. *How's that going to be enough for everyone?* I thought. *Perhaps they'd run out of milk?* Tipping carefully, trying to use the smallest splash I could that would make the coffee drinkable, I emptied half the jug. I pushed the incriminating evidence towards The Dane before I was labelled the milk bandit. Just as I was settling in for my coffee Lene, who'd excused herself from the table earlier, returned carrying an IKEA tray full of small white bread rolls. A selection of butter, cheese, cold meats, capsicum and chocolate slices were beautifully arranged on their own platter. The chocolate slices were a magical Danish invention that made chocolate on bread socially acceptable for all ages.

Turning the conversation back to me, as she placed the warm *bolle* (or bread rolls as I would have called them) on the table, Lene brought me back into the circle.

"How's language school going?"

"Good," I replied, not knowing how else to explain the soul-sucking experience of learning a language as a late bilingual bloomer.

"It's one of the hardest languages to learn in the world apparently" she replied.

"So everyone keeps telling me," I answered in tones that might have been interpreted as indifferent.

"Can you understand what we're talking about in Danish?"

"Some of it…" I began to reply before being cut off as they switched back into Danish, leaving me in a smiling nodding mess of confusion. *Clearly my optimistic report of my progress had been too positive,* I thought. Becoming restless, I excused myself to play with BBB on the floor as I wondered when these social occasions would become less awkward and more agreeable to my Kiwi DNA.

4:48pm

Like mushrooms, a selection of board games had mysteriously sprouted out of nowhere on the table, a sign that the final hygge hour was about to begin. *That'll take us to 6pm,* I thought. *Bang on three hours.* It wasn't hard to understand why coffee was served in thermal coffee pots in this country.

Two rounds of *Sequence* later, we made our way to the shoe and jacket depository room and began reclaiming our outerwear. I began wrestling BBB into her all-in-one outdoor suit, a *flyverdragt* as it was known in Danish.

"Thank you," Lars enthusiastically gushed with genuine warmth that made me almost feel guilty for my restlessness during the marathon coffee convention. "It was so *hyggeligt.*"

"You're coming to Camilla and Christian's birthday party, right?" Lene added.

I'd forgotten about that invitation. *Oh God, we're going to have to do this all over again, but even longer,* I thought. *Did I have another eight hours of socialising in me?* I wondered. If my memory served me right, that was the social engagement ringed in ink sometime next month on our family wall calendar.

Danes drink a lot of coffee. Most of it is from a filter machine, but increasing also from a barista. And a lot of them like it strong, the kind of strong that puts hairs on your chest. Milk can be a minimalistic optional accessory.

Ten, Dining With Danes

Birthday formalities

"Introduce yourself to everyone and shake their hand," briefed The Dane as we arrived at Camilla and Christian's brightly lit house on the outskirts of Copenhagen. Its obligatory flagpole stood to attention as it towered above the house like a drill sergeant posed to inspect the birthday party guests. *Hopefully we pass muster,* I thought.

I tilted my head, unsure whether I should be offended or merely amused at The Dane's explicit handshaking directive. The last time I'd been given a formal directive to shake someone's hand was 15 years earlier when I graduated from university. *Had I developed a reputation for social heathen tendencies if left to my own devices at Danish parties?* I wondered. I quickly reviewed my memory bank for possible misdemeanours at the few Danish social occasions we'd attended and came up with nothing.

Reaching through the hedge, I fumbled for the gate latch while doing my best not to drop the wishlist-approved present balancing in my other hand. To my amusement, the wishlist had been emailed to us along with the invitation. *Presumptuous,* I'd thought at the time.

"Remind me again why we had to buy a present from his wish-list," I asked The Dane.

"It's a round birthday."

"What's that again?" I asked as I kicked open the garden gate with perhaps a little too much force, and it slammed into the woody hedge behind it.

"When you turn 20, 30, 40 or 50, it ends in a round number. That's a round birthday."

"Never heard of it," I replied while asking myself if he was for real.

Round birthdays are a thing in Denmark. They're any birthday that ends in a round number, i.e. zero. 20, 30, 40, 50 and so on. Expect a party, flags, cake and possibly an amplified band.

Sent as a spreadsheet, the wishlist had been extremely detailed, with multiple columns clarifying the size, colour and suggested places where to buy each option. It even had back-up colour options. It was like a wedding register designed by an engineer for a grown-up's birthday. The Dane argued it was practical.

"Isn't it more meaningful if we hunt for something we think he'd like? You know, find something special?" I asked.

"Not if we end up buying him crap," came the short and hard-to-argue-with answer. And so, the wishlist-approved present had been The Dane's choice. A ridiculously expensive set of mini vases with stripes because they could do next day delivery.

Wishlists, or *ønskelister* as it's known in Danish, is the system where you write a list of what you want as a present for a significant occasion. Quite practical, but possibly a bit odd for those not brought up with the system. It's one of the reasons for mass returns at the shops post-celebration with often multiple people buying the same item from the wishlist. There is however now an App to manage this problem for those who choose to use it.

"Can you get BBB?" I yelled over my shoulder, more as a directive than a question at The Dane as I held the gate open. Since temporarily misplacing her at the *loppemarked* I took no chances.

Just like their names, Camilla and Christian went together like a horse and carriage. Walking along the winding cobblestone path, I took in the view of their whitewashed (inside and out) Instagram-mable Scandi-stylish home framed perfectly by the autumnal hedge. *Did I have time to take a photo?*

"Hurry up," The Dane interrupted, as he shunted me from behind with **BBB** in his arms. "It's 5:29pm."

Not this again, I huffed under my breath.

"The invite said it started at 5:30pm," I reminded him. I knew exactly when it started, because we'd received the invitation three months earlier and it had been hanging next to the oversized family calendar for 100 days. I'd committed every detail to heart. "We're on time."

"Exactly, hurry up. One more minute and we won't be," The Dane replied, lunging for the doorbell just as the clock struck

5:30pm. His sense of pride for being on time was almost palpable. Wisely, I resisted the urge to comment.

Thanks to the twin and curtainless windows on either side of Camilla and Christian's front door, the party (and their collection of Danish-designed, low hanging lamps together with their Arne Jacobsen-designed Egg™ chairs) was streaming live to anyone on the street who cared to peer in. Not that I saw anyone stopping. Passing pedestrians and neighbours walked on unbothered by the free show on display. *Danish furniture robbers must be the only ones who ever bother looking in these easily viewable house windows.*

I eyed the lamps wearily. Like moths to a flame, it would only be a matter of time before those bastards bumped me on the head, as they hung halfway between the ceiling and the floor.

There's an assumption living in Copenhagen that at some point you'll accidentally see your neighbour naked (and vice versa) due to apartment windows facing each other with curtains hardly ever used. Once that is out of the way, there's really not much else to see, which is maybe why no one bothers with looking into each other's apartments and no one feels the need to pull the curtains (or in some cases, even have them).

Interrupting my internal ramblings, the door swung open and Camilla and Christian greeted us with a simultaneous 'welcome' and 'come on in' salute. A round of handshakes and halfway hugs followed, during which I carefully retracted my lips and extended my cheeks once again in fear of the European kiss greeting. It wasn't normally a Danish thing, but nevertheless I thought it wise to remain on guard.

The skill of greeting the hosts while kicking off my shoes, shedding my winter jacket and finding a place for my handbag that neither caused a roadblock nor shoved my bum in someone's face was a skill I'd yet to master. Entrance rooms and de-robing procedures were not a situation I'd been trained for. I was not a natural in managing layers at this level while socialising, and found the colder months exasperating. I shoved the wishlist-approved gift into The Dane's hands in exchange for an already disrobed BBB now plopped at my feet. *How did he manage that so fast?* I sighed and bent down to remove my shoes. Beginning to overheat immediately, a small river of sweat trickled down my spine and began to turn my freshly straightened hair into a bird's nest. *Jacket off first* I reminded myself for next time.

Adding our shoes to the growing mountain now gathering at the doorway, I glimpsed a sea of sock-wearing feet belonging to a bunch of strangers making small talk in the next room. Lifting my gaze upwards from the talking socks, I surveyed the room for where I could get a drink before conquering the roomful of Danes.

"I'll just grab a drink," I replied.

"No. You need to introduce yourself first," The Dane insisted, with a strange amount of vocal emphasis on the word 'first'. Until now, the highlight of my social life had been the company of a bottle of New Zealand Sauvignon Blanc on our Hans Wegner Danish vintage sofa, or if we want to call a spade a spade, it could also be described as the '1970s sofa'. The Dane's repetitive social warnings were now beginning to make me doubt my social abilities. My brain went into overdrive: I guess I hadn't been out that much here yet. *Maybe I'm a heathen by local standards? I eat fast and often disregard* smørrebrød *rules. Maybe he is trying to redeem my sociability? Did I need redeeming? Possibly.*

"Of course I'll say *hej* to everyone, but I'll just grab a drink first. It'll take one sec," I said, reassuring myself it was a reasonable arrival strategy.

He walked away.

"Ohh. You mean right now?" I said to the back of his head as it disappeared towards the first group of sock-wearers huddled close together at the table. His arm was outstretched in front of him, ready for action.

"Yes, now. They're expecting you to shake hands," The Dane insisted, delivering the final protocol warning as he walked into the lounge, which had been turned into an extended dining room. That left me to sort myself out and find an indoor parking spot for our daughter.

I wondered whether I might need to make a speech too. I began mentally drafting it while settling BBB into the kids' corner. *Why the urgency for introductions?*

Aside from the designer furniture, the modernistic lighting, a plethora of stylish napkins and a small trailer-load of candles on the table, it seemed similar to a New Zealand party. But the compulsory handshaking on arrival was something new. It felt like a drill in formalities for meeting the Queen, except without the entourage at the entrance offering to take your coat while another one presented a tray your way with a glass of champagne on it. *Not that I'd ever been to such an event.*

My fear of being left alone in a room of foreign-speaking strangers was greater than my fear of introductions. I needed to follow quickly. Catching him up, I could see The Dane was already rippling like a wave through the room as he exchanged names and handshakes with a firm Viking grip. Sticking out my hand, I followed his lead.

"*Hej. Jeg hedder Johan,*" the tall and bearded Viking in front of me said as way of introduction.

"Hi. I'm Keri, how are you?" I replied, annoyingly brightly, as I decided to combat my nerves with a display of over-excitement. Standing in anticipation, I waited for bearded Viking's reply.

"Errrrr. Ja. Okay," he stuttered awkwardly, looking surprised at the question. I looked for The Dane to translate, but he was off, halfway around the room, arm outstretched as he shook, nodded, smiled and moved on with more efficiency than I thought necessary. It was clear he'd been doing this from birth.

Turning back, I was greeted with a newly outstretched arm, the previous Bearded Viking having taken a step to his left and moved to a 'safe' distance from my 'how are you?' inquisition.

Connected to the newly outstretched arm was a female Viking, towering above me even in her stockinged feet.

"*Hej. Jeg hedder Kirsten,*" she offered. *Wow. They all say the exact same thing.* I snickered to myself.

And so, the introductions continued hard and fast. Like a chorus of cicadas, formalities were soon taken care of. At some stage during the process, the standard introduction became abbreviated to an even shorter format of two words with a simple '*hej*' and their first name. The giver and receiver barely looked at each other. The shortened version resulted in the greeting becoming more like a statement made under duress without eye contact rather than an introduction of warmth.

The conveyer belt of introductions continued. Finally, I reached the last person in the room: the Danish wildcard who, ignoring the pattern set before him, brazenly introduced himself using both names,

"*Hej. Jeg hedder Henrik Henriksen.*"

With such a delightful name I was tempted to go off script too and add my surname to my greeting. I had a feeling Henrik was going to be my favourite party guest for the evening.

But right now, I *really* needed a drink. I spotted The Dane moving towards the kitchen where the sleek floor-to-ceiling cabinetry lined the walls with every major appliance hidden away. The only sign of colour was the industrial sized Kenwood mixer bowl – an injection of deep red against the white of the cabinets. It was a statement piece. An impressive-looking rubbish bin was the only other asset on display in the kitchen and had the word 'vipp' printed across the top. *I must look that up,* I thought to myself, intrigued how a rubbish bin had caught my attention.

Vipp pedal bins are the designer rubbish bin you didn't know you needed.
In 1939, Holger Nielsen, a young Danish metalworker, was asked by his wife to design a sturdy pedal-controlled bin for her hairdressing salon. A design that lead to many more accessories as well as furniture and was even a catalyst for a design hotel concept.
It's still a family-owned, independent, Danish design company now run by Holger's daughter, Jette Egelund, her two children Kasper and Sofie, together with 45 employees in Copenhagen.

"Where are the drinks?" I asked, staring at the glaring but sadly bare white surfaces.

Apart from a string of twinkly fairy lights over the kitchen bench, there was nothing.

"Outside," The Dane answered, opening the backdoor onto the small deck and momentarily disappearing before returning with two Carlsbergs.

"That's a Danish fridge," he explained. "Colder outside than the temperature in the fridge," he continued in response to my questioning eyebrows. "So, we just put the beers outside. You haven't seen that before?"

From my vantage point next to the hidden built-in fridge, I could hear the repetitive speed-handshaking greeting ritual beginning again with the arrival of the next set of guests. Watching from a safe distance, I realised speed rather than small talk was the essence of the exercise.

"Do you remember anyone's name?" I asked The Dane as we drank our beers watching over BBB, who had found a hulking box of *LEGO®* to amuse herself with.

"Some."

Well, that's more than me, I mused. *Apart from Henrik Henriksen.*

When arriving at a social gathering in Denmark you'll be expected to go around the room shaking everybody's hand and introducing yourself, using the well-drilled phrase of *'Hej, jeg hedder ...'* (Hi, my name is). Just like those red and white introduction stickers used in the 1980s. A smile or a hello from a distance is not considered adequate. Nor is a friendly Kiwi eyebrow raise.

After completing the conveyer belt of handshakes, do not expect anyone to remember your name.

Failure to shake hands will result in being labelled odd and rude.

Bonus insight: Arrive early, make the newly arrived guests come to you and avoid having to shake 50 or more hands in a row.

The Six-hour Table Party

"I thought you said it was a party?" I asked as I sat next to The Dane, trying my best not to become too entranced by the plethora of table linen and accessories on the table in front of me. The matching, woodland-green themed napkins and tablecloth set off the small army of tea lights that ran the length of the table. Dotted at perfect intervals between the lights were glorious salt and pepper shakers and curvaceous water bottles. *Now I understand why they sell entire pallets of tea light candles at the supermarket,* I thought as the mystery of Danish supermarket shopping became a bit clearer.

A nuclear bomb-sized arrangement of flowers exploded from a glass vase in the middle of the table.

"I presume there are more guests seated on the other side of the flowers?" I asked The Dane in jest, to which there was no reply.

"It is a party," The Dane insisted.

"Looks more like a State Banquet to me," I quipped. "Why so formal?" I asked in an attempt to gain my social bearings.

"It's not. It's normal."

"It is?" I said, raising my hands questioningly in a Sherlock Holmes fashion at the Rosendahl table collection laying in front of us. "Everyone has a seat."

This wasn't the free-range party format I was used to, where guests would stick out their chests in confidence, drink in hand, circulating the room, jumping from one conversation to the next. Once bored with the company of one person they made a beeline for the next interesting interaction. At my previous New Zealand parties, a seat was defined as anywhere you could place your bum. The arm of a sofa, the hallway steps or sitting on a retaining wall, all locations were valid seating options. No one expected a seat at a table. *If only Danish parties came with briefing notes.*

"Well, of course they have a seat, we're eating," replied The Dane, mystified with my logic. "You can't eat sitting on a couch."

Actually... in some parts of the world that's how we do it. My thoughts were swiftly interrupted by the arrival of Henrik Henriksen who plonked himself down on my left, politely nodding at me in acknowledgement as he did so.

In the distance, behind the miniature forest in the middle of the table, I watched Bearded Viking hurriedly find a seat at the opposite side of the table as far away as possible from me. I was hopeful he'd work through his awkwardness after a few beers.

"Don't take too much," instructed The Dane as I began to serve myself from one of the many platters of food on the table.

Was he serious or plain stupid? I wondered as I considered once again my heathen status.

"Is there a ration system in place?" I enquired slowly while glancing over at the Danish wildcard Henrik Henriksen's plate to inspect the state of his portion control.

"No – it's because you eat fast," the Dane whispered back.

I do? I asked myself as I sucked in a breath to best absorb the feedback while holding on to the fact he said fast and not fat.

"There's more food coming, so you don't need to put it all on your plate at once. You're not in New Zealand now. And don't take the meat first," he instructed as I placed two pieces of pork loin on my plate. *Too late.*

I was drawing a blank at the reference to New Zealand eating techniques but took some solace in the fact The Dane wasn't signing me up for Weight Watchers or enlisting me in a Boot Camp, just yet.

To best blend in at a Danish table, your eating speed and portion sizes should be slow and small. And always take the fish dish first.

I looked at my watch, we were one hour in and had barely made a dent in the food as dishes continued to be added to the table. The writing was on the wall that we were heading towards a five-hour minimum eating fest. I could feel my legs itch with the desire to be stretched, as if in anticipation of having to be seated in the same place for another four hours. *This is like flying long haul,* I thought. I willed my face to remain open and interested among the murmur of Danish around me.

Placing the final piece of asparagus on my plate into my mouth, I saw I was the only one with an empty plate at the table. Despite my best efforts, I'd misjudged the tempo of the occasion. I'd tried so hard to replicate Henrik Henriksen's portions and eating pace and I'd still screwed up. *Now what do I do?* I wondered as I stared at my clean plate while the talkative guests around me all still had plenty to keep them going. Not wanting to be the first to reach for more food, I began rearranging my now damp napkin and unnecessarily filling my water glass, along with anyone else's I could reach, without having to ask them for it. I refilled my wine glass. It took, at best, three minutes.

"There's quite a lot of people like you around, isn't there?" I asked Henrik Henriksen.

Dropping his water glass, a small river formed across the table navigating the trail of tealights. Impressively none extinguished. *Did I do that?* I grabbed the woodland-green napkins in an attempt to soak up the pooling water, while slightly thrilled I had found a job to fill in another three minutes of sitting at the table.

"A lot of me?" Henrik spluttered seeking clarification. "Do you mean Danes?"

"Well, yes and no. Danes with double names like yours is what I meant." I tried to clarify, "Lars Larsen, Anders Andersen, oh, and there was a politician too – what was his name?"

"I'm not a politician."

"I know, I was just saying, I see quite a lot of Danish names that do that double-up thing. You hadn't noticed?" I continued, with the enthusiasm only a person who finds themself in a hole can muster.

"No."

With my level of social awkwardness rising to new levels, and all hope of Henrik Henriksen being my saving grace in the small talk department fading, it felt like a good time to excuse myself from the table.

"Sorry, I just need to check on my daughter. I'll be back in a minute," I said, not that she needed looking after; the baby monitor hidden in my pocket had remained silent since I'd tucked her into a portable bed in an upstairs bedroom.

Jumping up, I felt the sharp edge of the expensive-looking, low hanging designer lamp hit the side of my head. My fellow dining companions lunged forward with remarkable co-ordination in an attempt to steady the swaying candelabra, which had momentarily foiled my escape route.

The Dane looked on. "What are you doing?"

"I'm not sure. Back soon," I whispered, rushing to safety.

Locking the bathroom door behind me, I relaxed for a few minutes and contemplated how long I could stay hidden for. *Probably not that long*, I thought as I calculated the odds of someone else needing to use the toilet between now and midnight. But for one brief moment, I enjoyed my refuge from the Danish marathon food fest taking place beyond the bathroom walls.

After checking every social feed I owned, including even my LinkedIn account, I sent a quick message to a friend in New Zealand and told her I was hiding in the bathroom. I looked at my watch. Fifteen minutes had passed; my hygge time-out session had maxed out. I returned to the table.

"What are these?" I asked The Dane as I sat back at the table and found a sheet of paper at my place.

"Song sheets. We'll be starting soon."

Fark me. Singing? I suppose it had to happen sooner or later, I thought. Danes loved a good singsong. I'd experienced this phenomenon before, but was now cursing the timing of my return from the bathroom refuge. *If only I'd stayed in there another half-hour, I would have missed this.*

Højskolesangbogen, the High School Songbook, is the most popular songbook in Denmark. The songs in the book are a mix of Danish folksongs and hymns. The first edition was published in 1888 and the 19th edition in November 2020. In the latest edition there are now 601 songs, 151 of which are new. Its enduring popularity is almost certainly the reason for the strong Danish love of communal singing.

Fortifying myself, I filled my water glass and downed it in one hit pretending it was vodka. Grabbing the small, party-sized Danish flag that had been left as a gift on my seat (the universal sign of celebration in Denmark) I declared my readiness to no one in particular – not that anyone was listening anyway. I resigned myself to another session of Danish songs, of which I knew neither the music nor the words. I was buoyed by the realisation that half the guests around me also appeared to be struggling as an awkward 25 minutes of my life played out before my eyes.

Many hours later, I zipped a sleeping BBB into in her thermal lined cycle-trailer bag and congratulated myself on surviving the Viking dining rituals.

"Are they all like that?" I asked The Dane as we headed home along the cycle lane.

"Organised, you mean?"

"Formal and long," I corrected.

"Well, you'll always have a seat at a Danish party, if that's what you mean," The Dane offered. "And you'll always get good use out of it."

"It was a long time to sit in one seat," was all I could muster as a reply. "But at least we didn't have to dance around a Christmas tree, I suppose."

"Don't worry. That's coming," The Dane replied.

Denmark has a list of preapproved names that parents must use to name their offspring. The names are divided into three lists. 1. Boys' names 2. Girls' names and 3. Unisex names. A boy's name can't be given to a girl, and vice versa. If you want to use a name that isn't on the list, then you'll need to apply for special permission.

Dancing Around the Christmas Tree

I was sandwiched between two enthusiastic Vikings who, like me, wore shades of red and green with a splash of gold. Our hands were awkwardly linked forming a human chain encircling the Christmas tree. I wondered what the rules were for the firmness of grip in these situations as my fingers began cramping. It brought to mind awkward memories of compulsory folk dancing at school as an eight-year-old.

Like a ragdoll, my arms were being tugged in both directions by my companions who tried their best to show me in which direction I should be dancing. Although dancing seemed a fancy way to describe our motions. At best we were taking a brisk, albeit drunk, walk around the Christmas tree. Was it obvious that I wanted to run away? The Vikings' grips tightened while I tried my best to sing in a language I didn't speak.

If there was a scientific equation for measuring just how far one was outside one's comfort zone, I was pretty sure I was beyond the outer perimeter. This was almost on par with the communal showering experience at a Danish swimming pool. I wondered where I'd gone wrong with my life choices.

Naturally, I hadn't believed The Dane when he'd told me his family danced around the Christmas tree on Christmas Day (which was really Christmas Eve in my world – the 24th of December). I thought he'd been joking, indulging in a Viking tale to scare me and the rest of the foreigners – like when I'd tell tourists in New Zealand they could drive from the North to the South Island.

I'd marvelled – when we first arrived – at why someone would put a tree in the middle of the floor. I was woefully under-prepared for a Christmas in Denmark.

Across from me, The Dane was in full flight. Charging the tree from both directions, stepping to the left and right, while gripping his songbook like a winning Lottery ticket. His ability to hold hands plus have the book wedged between his fingers was impressive. I was trying to do the same, but with the grace of an elephant attempting ballet. *What I'd give to be upstairs tucked up in bed with BBB right now,* I whimsically wished. I thought back to the seated, hour-long birthday-fest of sock-wearers at Camilla and Christian's. It'd been good training for my first Christmas in Denmark, but it hadn't been enough. How could anything ever prepare you for this phenomenon? I'd just emerged from a multi-hour Christmas feast at the dining room table. My bum had gone numb halfway through and, though I was dreading it, being released to dance around the Christmas tree had been a welcome escape. *I could have flown halfway to Hawaii in that time,* I mused.

We'd started with coffee which at some point merged into the beginning of the meal, ending several hours later with a hunt for an almond in a bowl of rice. During this time I'd learnt that brown and white potatoes were critical to the success of a Danish Christmas and that brown potatoes were actually caramelised potatoes, potatoes cooked in sugar. In one of the many toilet breaks I'd engineered over those long hours at the table, I checked my social media feeds looking for signs of life to keep me going only to discover my feed full of identical food photos from others in Denmark. Everyone was eating brown and white potatoes and hunting for a bloody almond. It was as if the Danish rule book issued everyone with a 'set menu'. Now I knew why my suggestion of bringing along the Kiwi traditional Christmas pavlova had brought confused looks. Meringue was not on the menu in Denmark.

Until now, I'd thought that surviving the intense lead-up to Christmas had been the hard part. Two months of surviving the shops and endless social occasions. Stores had been full of mountains of Christmas cookies, Christmas *Nisser* (a type of elf) and Christmas-themed napkins. Streets had been overtaken with Christmas markets and suffocated with strings of twinkly lights. Together with the seasons, occasions to celebrate were a big thing in Vikingland. It was only possible to miss Christmas in Denmark if you were in a coma.

Spinning around the tree for the 100th time, I focussed on the lit candles on the tree. In the middle of the room? *Wild*, I thought. Small flames and a bunch of tipsy adults heartily singing with such conviction they barely noticed the potential danger in front of us. I looked around for the emergency bucket of water to douse the tree should it ignite. Nothing.

I gripped my songbook, not because I could read it, but because it felt good to grip on to something, anything. I stared at it with an overabundance of hope, praying it would give me some clue as to what was about to come next. This was a flawed strategy, of course, given it was written in Danish and because my dancing companions seemed to be jumping from one page to the next in no particular order.

"Are there many more songs to come?" I asked the dancing Viking beside me, hoping the question didn't sound too desperate.

"There's four more songs to go," he yelled back while nodding at the almighty Christmas songbook.

Could I fake an ankle sprain? I wondered, analysing the inebriated state of my fellow tree-dancers while considering how to call a hygge time-out.

Grabbing my chance in a lull between songs, I made a break for it, leaving them to continue debating which song would be next.

"I'm just going to take some photos," I announced, extracting myself from the web of Viking hands and songbooks. *And maybe some video too. No one at home would understand unless they saw it.* I made myself look busy at the back of the room.

Sometime later the momentum waned. A small nugget of hope rose in me. It might be wrapping up.

"Shall we open the presents now?" one of the elders suggested.

"Is it always done in this order? Dancing first then presents?" I asked The Dane, who had joined me on the sofa as we waited for the distribution of gifts.

"Yes, it's Christmas," he answered, not giving me any further insight to the schedule of events. Right from the beginning, the day felt upside down with us celebrating a day too early. In my previous life, the 24th of December was for mad sprints to the supermarket in search of fresh cream and strawberries, and any other last-minute ingredients that had somehow been forgotten in the lead up to Christmas. It was also a day to buy the final Christmas presents and get drunk with your friends at the local pub – and maybe go to the beach and have a barbeque. It wasn't a day to hold hands with my family and dance around a lit Christmas tree.

Watching the mass present-reveal, I noticed that no one seemed surprised or excited by their gifts. Strangely, more than one person had received identical items.

"Did they all know what they were getting?" I asked The Dane for clarity.

"Probably. It would have been on their wishlists," he replied.

"Wishlists for Christmas too?" I marvelled.

Collapsing onto the bed later, I congratulated myself on making it through the evening.

"That was intense," I stuttered, realising it was nearly 2am. "Good night."

"*God nat,*" The Dane offered in return. "Just New Year's to go now," he said, before lying flat and snoring at the same time his head hit the pillow.

Was New Year's going to be the same? He couldn't be serious. For the love of God, let's not do this for another 12 months, I silently pleaded.

Some Danish families serve bowls of potato chips (crisps or *franske kartofler*) alongside the main Christmas meal. They are not your entrée, nor a snack to have with your Christmas beer. They are part of your main dish. Knock yourself out. Copenhageners will either tell you they've never heard of it, or that it's just those in Jutland (another part of Denmark) who do this. But they'll be wrong (or in denial). It's a little tradition that has now spread around the country into other quarters. If you fancy giving it a go, just know that there are only two types of acceptable chips to choose from: either 'Taffel Original Franske Kartofler' or 'Meny Pariser Chips'. Stray from those and you'll be in for a socially awkward moment.

Grab Your Hat

The harsh, fluorescent supermarket lighting was making it impossible to get a decent selfie. Moving along the aisle in search of a better spot, I tried my best to blend in. Not that anyone seemed bothered by my antics – most shoppers were predictably pretending they couldn't see me. Other than little old ladies fascinated by BBB, spontaneous interactions and conversations with strangers remained uncommon in the supermarket.

Pushing BBB to the end of the aisle in search of more favourable light, I parked her out of the way before turning my full attention back to the giant bin of novelty hats I'd discovered. Digging with the enthusiasm of a schoolgirl high on sugar for the next gem to try on, I pulled a giant pink flamingo over my head.

"Are they really only 40 kroner?" I asked The Dane, who was standing at the other end of the aisle pretending he didn't know me.

"Yes," he patiently replied, knowing better than to try and hurry me as I delighted in this unexpected Danish peculiarity.

"What are they for?" I asked, taking the flamingo off and pulling an oversized red-and-yellow French fries carton over my head. Fries exploded from the sides of my head in a Pippi-Longstocking pigtails-on-steroids kind of fashion. *Maybe it was an end-of-year clean out?* I surmised.

"They're hats for New Year's Eve," The Dane explained flatly.

"Hats for New Year's Eve? That's a thing?" I asked. "For everyone?" I looked again at the spectacular selection of tacky and sequined dress-up hats in front of me.

"Sure. For everyone who wants to."

I couldn't help but smile. Vikingland was one surprise after another.

"You don't just get drunk and fall asleep before midnight?" I asked, sensing this was an important cultural lesson to prepare myself for my first New Year's Eve in Denmark.

"That might happen, but it's not normal," he replied. "At least not before midnight."

The Dane had started to brief me the night before about what to expect at the New Year's Eve party we'd been invited to, but at some point in between the warnings of a three-course meal, the Queen's speech, fireworks, jumping off couches and an odd English short film called *Dinner for One*, the words had fused together into white noise.

"Why didn't you tell me about the hats too?" I asked, knowing that stories of burly bearded Vikings wearing flamingos on their heads would have caught my attention. "These are brilliant."

Continuing my enthusiastic research, I tried on several more, taking a selfie of each before heading to the self-service checkout with three hats and a large bag of indoor fireworks – something The Dane had insisted we buy for the big night.

"What exactly are indoor fireworks?" I asked as we headed home on foot, mystified with his love of all things explosive.

"You'll see," he exclaimed.

When the Sky Exploded

"Is this the madness you meant?" I asked staring out the front door as another rocket whizzed past. Indoor fireworks were, it seemed, the least of my worries on New Year's Eve as I stood staring at their outdoor pyrotechnic cousins. The explosions were continuous and with more punch and spark than I'd ever seen in a suburban setting.

"That's nothing. Wait until it hits midnight," The Dane replied excitedly. It was the most animated I'd seen him all year.

Bracing myself, I took a tentative step with BBB onto the street at precisely the same time as a recreational rocket exploded above our heads. The ferocity and frequency of the fireworks were in a different league to anything available in New Zealand, where they also weren't the main form of entertainment on New Year's Eve. Placing rockets in unsteady champagne bottles seemed to be the preferred launching method in Vikingland. *That'll be the real reason why champagne is such a big seller this time of the year,* I mused while nervously staring at the very surreal scene in front of me. Scandi Sameville had gone feral.

Crikey. They're pissed too, I realised as I took in the scene before me. Looking towards The Dane I hoped he'd give me a heads up if we were in danger. *Was this normal behaviour?* I shot him a querying look.

In response, I got nothing. Not even a flinch. His tailored suit, complete with tie and safety goggles, now looked not nearly as ridiculous as it had five minutes earlier inside the apartment. His nonchalant resilience to the unsupervised firework-fest happening above our heads was at complete odds to mine. My mouth hung open in fear, while his gaped wide in glee, as we both stared upwards at the dark sky being lit up by a steady supply of rockets that seemed to be coming from every direction. This was not a night for the faint-hearted.

The sky had been exploding over our heads (most were legal fireworks, some not) for the last two hours. I looked at my watch. *5:28pm.*

Gawd it's not even 6 o'clock yet, I contemplated, wondering how much longer it could go on for.

Gripping BBB's pram harder, I quickened my pace while cursing my decision not to buy my own safety goggles.

"Let's go!" I shouted to The Dane over my shoulder. "Before we get a rocket up our jacksies."

Normally it was a comfortable 700m walk to our friend's house, but tonight my heart rate suggested it was much further. My anxiety level increased with every footstep and explosion.

Crossing the road, I saw two young Vikings, likely in their 20s, drinking beer, with cartons of exploded fireworks the size of beer crates at their feet.

"*Godt Nytår!*" They beamed at us as they took a pause from their pyromaniac urges.

"That's never happened before," I said to The Dane.

"What?"

"Strangers saying 'hello'. That never happens in Copenhagen," I replied. "Do you think they're alright?"

"Well, they're drunk. But otherwise I think they're fine."

I mentally clapped my hands together. Finally, I'd found the one night of the year where I fitted in, when my unique talent of talking to strangers was acceptable in Vikingland. Loosening my grip on the pram a little, I felt a tad bolder for the rest of the walk, embracing the random greetings flung in our direction as we passed strangers on their way to their parties. These were people I'd never met before and was likely to never talk to again.

"Woah. What happened to that?" I asked, pointing at a hunk of metal ripped into shreds sitting on a post where someone's letterbox should have been.

"Letterbox fireworks," The Dane replied. "They drop fireworks in it to see how much damage it can make. The owners must have forgotten to put a bowl of water in there," he explained as if it was the fault of the owner that their letterbox had been destroyed in a New Year's Eve science experiment.

These Vikings are batshit crazy, I concluded.

Reaching our destination, The Dane pressed the doorbell while we hovered anxiously to be buzzed in. The city dwellers' skyrockets continued raining down around us.

"They're Pedersen and Petersen?!" I exclaimed in pure delight as I spotted their surnames on the letterbox. "Two different surnames?"

"Yes, I've told you that before," The Dane replied.

"Always sounded the same to me," I replied as we were buzzed into the stairwell.

"Quick – the hats!" I ordered, as I began digging in our New Year's survival bag for the dress-up hats I'd brought at the super-market. I pulled a turquoise fish with glitter fins over BBB's head just in time as the door opened.

"Is their dog okay?" I asked The Dane after completing the conveyor-belt round of handshakes with BBB, who was still more a waddler than a walker, on my hip. I noticed my ability to manage the entry formalities was improving as I nearly effortlessly disrobed my outer garments.

"What's that?" The Dane enquired.

"Doesn't the dog look a bit, ummm, stoned?" I asked as I watched it do a four-legged saunter in a circle before eyeballing me and collapsing in slow motion in the kitchen corner.

"They've probably drugged it," The Dane replied as he excitedly tugged on a New Year's cracker, with the dog winking slowly in return.

"A drugged dog? Is that a thing too?" I asked unsure if I should be amused or shocked. Nervously, I straightened my glittery New Year's top hat as the dog continued watching me with an unnerving semi-grin spread across its muzzle.

"Hurry, the Queen's speech is about to start!" Pedersen called, ushering us into the lounge while the dog remained in his chillaxed happy place.

"Quick – what colour is her dress going to be?" a scaringly over-enthusiastic Viking, whose name I couldn't remember, yelled from the grey sofa that was drowning in decorative cushions. Pedersen and Petersen, as I enjoyed calling them (although not to their faces), together with the remaining Vikings, began yelling their colour picks at the TV screen. The Danish names for the colours didn't help my understanding of who was backing what.

"*Blå!*" yelled my date for the night with an unnerving amount of enthusiasm, causing BBB to jump in my lap.

"Blue?" I queried as he nodded back in confirmation at me. His eyes on stalks watched the TV with great excitement to see who was right, even though, to my knowledge, no money had changed hands. *They must just be playing for bragging rights,* I guessed.

New Year's Eve celebrations in Denmark begin at 6pm with a glass of champagne while watching the Queen's speech. The private use of fireworks, however, will start much earlier and go on for much longer.

Bonus insight: Run a sweepstake with your guests, guessing what colour dress the Queen will be wearing. Or for the more advanced, create bingo cards with everything the Queen might mention in her speech.

Sitting in silence, staring bug-eyed at the television screen, I realised there was a ceasefire outside. It seemed even those responsible for the urban explosions paused for the occasion. The Vikings intently hung on their Queen's every word. *This is some weird shit,* I thought to myself, hoping no one could see my face as my nose and eyebrows raised in tandem trying to make sense of what was happening.

"Have they had some of what the dogs had?" I whispered to The Dane next to me who chose to ignore my question. Unable to understand any of the Queen's speech, I instead busied myself emptying my glass of wine. It seemed like a sombre occasion, in direct contrast to the circus of dynamite that had been in full throttle outside the window a few minutes earlier.

Watching Queen Margrethe II, I couldn't help but compare her to my Queen, Elizabeth II – the Commonwealth's Queen – who now in her 90s probably looked at this Danish spring chicken in her late 70s with bemusement. The Vikingland Queen's speech notes were stapled together just how I used to do at school.

"Why are her notes stapled?" I asked The Dane. "Do you not have teleprompters?"

"The cards got mixed up one year, so now she staples them," The Dane shared.

"But why cards? Surely she's got access to some better technology," I replied. "It looks like she's presenting a school debate."

The room of Vikings collectively gasped. Perhaps they were not the right crowd to share my thoughts with after all. I knew the warm-up wine had loosened my tongue so I bit it, hard. I looked back at the television just in time to see Margrethe II of Denmark pull a tissue from her sleeve and blow her nose. On the telly! Knock me down with a feather duster.

"THE QUEEN BLEW HER NOSE ON THE TELLY," I roared to The Dane in disbelief. "My queen would never do that. God, this is brilliant entertainment." I exclaimed to myself.

"She had a snotty nose," The Dane replied, unrattled by the commoner behaviour as he swirled his empty champagne glass.

"Wine-opener? Where is it?" shouted Pedersen in a panic, waking me from my royal coma before disappearing out the front door to try his luck at the neighbours'. Neighbours that I knew he never talked to at any other time of the year. He seemed breathlessly panicked. New Year's Eve appeared to be the only time when talking to strangers was encouraged. Running back into the apartment a few minutes later he threw a wine-opener to Petersen, who in one fluid movement opened the bottle of wine that was sitting next to the champagne on a silver tray in front of us, just as their Queen finished her speech.

"Aren't we supposed to be drinking champagne for this bit?" I queried before I was drowned out.

"*Skål!*" someone yelled at the end of the royal performance as the Vikings enthusiastically downed their bubbles and the other expensive looking bottle. They then began to dissect the speech in detail.

What the hell just happened? I wondered with a feeling that I'd just witnessed some sort of ritual. I gave myself a pinch under my arm to make sure I wasn't dreaming. Migrating back to the dining room table with its black tablecloth and confetti canon contents scattered over it, I checked on the dog, who was at least looking a little less stoned. Sitting down after putting **BBB** to bed, I settled in for another six-hour event. I was much more match-fit this time after the last few months of social engagements. This would be the final social experiment in my three-month long crash course of how to socialise with Vikings. *Would I be eligible for an award? Would I get a survivors shirt? Will my efforts be noted in my integration contract?*

Three slow and long courses later, I realised it didn't seem as painful this time. Maybe it was the wine?

"Let's do the indoor fireworks," The Dane excitedly suggested to the table of his fellow Vikings as he looked at his watch. *As if the outdoor fireworks weren't enough?* I asked myself, *these guys also created an indoor option?* I remained sceptical.

Within minutes, the table became awash with a deluge of metallic confetti that I suspected the hosts would still be finding months later. It was truly remarkable that **BBB** was sleeping through all of this in the spare room. *Yet another marvel of the Viking DNA.*

Dinner for One is a British-German film recorded in 1963 that enjoys a cult status in Denmark (as well as Germany). Virtually unknown in the English-speaking world, it's an integral part of the New Year's Eve celebrations to observe. Played without fail on TV just before midnight every year. The film's most famous line – "Same procedure as last year?" – is often bantered about by Danes who call the film '*90-års fødselsdagen*'. Overall, it's a perplexing tradition and best to have had a few before you watch it.

11:34pm

"It's time," Pedersen announced, ushering us back into the lounge. He was definitely the whip cracker of the group, ensuring we were hitting the New Year's Eve milestones.

"For what?" I asked The Dane.

"*Dinner for One.*"

"What's that?"

"Everyone knows it," he replied.

"Not me; not everyone," I corrected.

"You'll see," he continued as we resumed our sitting positions in front of the television for Round Two. A new tray of champagne and glasses were placed on the white-oak coffee table in the middle of the room. Next to it stood a circular pyramid of doughnut-looking cakes with white squiggles on top. *That must be the marzipan thing he warned me about,* as some previous preamble came to mind.

I had long passed my limit of alcohol for the evening, but continued sipping on my wine as I tried to understand what was so important about the grainy black-and-white sketch on the TV in front of me. The Danes in the room roaring in laughter as an elderly waiter tripped on a tiger head while serving dinner to an elderly lady and her imaginary friends. The film was as weird as it sounded.

"Wow. What the hell is that?" I yelled, as the clock struck midnight and every inch of the sky erupted with exploding rockets putting to shame the night's earlier displays.

"You can't even buy these types of fireworks in New Zealand," I told the Dane as my mouth hung open in disbelief, yet again. "It's…" I began before pausing to find the right word: "wild."

Grabbing their supermarket-issue safety glasses, the pack of inebriated Vikings ran out to the small balcony, champagne flutes in hand.

"Is it always like this?" I asked The Dane, unsure if he could hear me as I placed a protective hand over my face, feeling very much nothing like a Dane and more like someone that had just lost their fireworks virginity.

"Every year," he confirmed, as my mouth fell open wider as if waiting for a rocket to land in it. *I need some of what the dog's got,* I thought.

Made with marzipan, *Kransekage* is a special cake eaten at midnight on New Year's Eve in Denmark. Best washed down with a glass of Champagne (especially if you're not a marzipan fan).

Eleven, Dating a Dane

Changing Seasons

Early in the New Year, after the celebratory gunpowder subsided, I resumed my search for hygge.

The dark wintry days of January had been chasing the locals indoors in droves to (if I was to believe the hype on hygge), hover around their thermal coffee pots, light tea candles and admire their designer lamps. Following suit, I experimented to see whether the days would pass faster the more pastries I ate.

Appreciation of my Danish 'must-have' *Rains* rain jacket (as described by the sales assistant who sold it to me), grew in equal measure with my gratitude that The Dane had chosen an apartment just 500m from a bakery. I was still trying to decide which to be more grateful for, even if, as I suspected, one of them was the reason for the expanding waistline I'd been ignoring. My jeans had become increasingly snug of late, testing the technologically advanced stretch denim to the limit. But I refused to let anyone, especially myself, blame the pastries. I'd seen others complain of the same phenomenon: *Danish jeans just aren't made for cycling*, I reasoned when the second inside-seam split in spectacular fashion while cycling to school.

But despite the bleakness of the season, I'd managed to make two friends, which I took as progress even if neither of them were Danish. It gave me someone other than just the supermarket cashier to smile at, which I sensed he was equally relieved about.

Then something remarkable happened. Like a shot of nirvana to my soul, the flora and fauna began to explode into life in the communal garden. I sent a small prayer of thanks to Mother Nature for the green splashes. There was hope. It also helped to neutralise The Dane's bright-green dining room wall that still blinded me as I reminded myself it'd look better once we found the right artwork for it.

Like cranky bears emerging from their winter slumber, the garden began to lure our neighbours back outside. It felt like it was the start of something new. My previously perceived privacy violation of having my name plastered on our letterbox for the world to see no longer shocked me. And aside from one failed attempt to purchase *koldskål*, a type of cold milky soup I wasn't entirely sure I needed in my life, I was tantalizingly close to being proficient navigating the dairy section of the supermarket. But there were still many things I had yet to master. Important stuff, like remembering never to take that last mouthful of my cup of tea unless I wanted a limescale mouthwash. *That's the sort of thing they should warn you about before moving to Vikingland,* I'd decided, imagining how much more useful my integration contract would have been had it warned me of that. But best of all would've been a heads up about the eye-watering fine I'd been given for forgetting to set the Parking Meter in the car. The fine wasn't for parking beyond the time limit, but just for not setting the Parking Meter. I'd cried that day. We were a bit more primitive in New Zealand with parking wardens who used chalk on tyres to mark how long cars had been parked. Knowing these things, as well as having a few more friends, would've made a difference as

I learned how to live in a country that wasn't mine. Even with the nurturance of world-class pastries, it had been a year of survival navigating the land of hygge. A state that I had begun to wonder would ever be obtainable to me as a foreigner in Denmark. I wondered if hygge was actually a clever way of keeping the non-Danes, out – a control mechanism to ensure everyone's behaviour was up to scratch. Although was this difficult to replicate state for foreigners, any more peculiar than when I used New Zealand slang? Would only those with the endurance to sit around a dining room table for six hours or enthusiastically eat rye bread until their twilight years be the only ones able to flourish in Denmark? *Surely my integration success wasn't dependent on a loaf of bread or a handshake, was it?*

Koldskål is a type of cold summer soup with a variety of 'goodies' you can throw into it. Things like small biscuits named *kammerjunkere*, strawberries and even bananas if you are feeling particularly wild.
Koldskål is best served as a lazy dinner on a hot summer night or as an afternoon snack.

Sandwiches With no Names

"Can you pass the bread?" I asked The Dane, purposefully avoiding the need to say *rugbrød*, a word I still couldn't pronounce and increasingly doubted I'd ever be able to. *BBB'll be saying it before I can,* I decided, resigning myself to the fact the mini-sized human sitting in a nappy next to me would soon run rings around my vocal cords.

Bread cutting was also something I fully expected never to master. Whereas The Dane's ability to slice a brick of rye bread was effortless and resulted in perfect slices of LEGO® precision every time. His technique was as mesmerising as watching a hot knife cut through butter. Exemplary slices that only magnified my own unfortunate, slices of door-wedge proportions. I speculated that my non-European DNA lacked the essential bread-cutting molecules, having grown up with a chest freezer fill of sliced bread that fulfilled all my daily requirements. Happily giving up on the bread quest, I relied instead on The Dane for my sliced bread needs.

I perched on my chair at our elliptical, Piet Hein-designed table. Its shiny metal legs and glossy top had the obligatory low hanging saucer lamp above it; I mentally applauded ourselves on the slow transformation from our previously sparse apartment. We even had a dust-collecting wooden monkey hanging from the ceiling. Made by a Danish designer whose name I could never remember, I took it as a sign we were well on our way of moving into the 'collecting unnecessary crap' stage of setting up a home.

Kay Bojesen is one of Denmark's most famous designers and is responsible for the multitude of decorative wooden monkeys hanging in Danish households. Created in 1951, it is widely known as the **Kay Bojesen's Monkey**.

Reaching into the wooden breadbasket, I could see The Dane was nervous before I'd even put a slice of the rye brick on my plate. His sideways glance and short sentences told me he was bracing for today's bread misdemeanour as I eyed the usual suspects on the table. We were having a lazy dinner tonight: rye bread and toppings. It reminded me that our debate regarding the naming of multigrain bread being brown or white was still unfinished. I'd found a few cafés tarting up rye bread, toasting and smashing avocado on it, turning it into something that looked a bit more exciting, albeit in another realm from the everyday, grassroots rye-feast in front of me. Not that I hated the stuff, it just didn't excite me.

Next to the rugbrød, a tub of Lurpak stared back at me. Cucumber, curried herrings, boiled eggs, cold potatoes, salami and mayonnaise circling like a bunch of high-school friends promising to hang out for eternity. I rarely saw these food musketeers making a solo debut. Each knew their place and, of most importance, the order in which to be placed on the bread. In an aluminium container, a mud-coloured liver paté concoction known to the locals as *leverpostej* stood like a teenage misfit – the rank outsider I hadn't yet been able to convince myself to touch, let alone taste. This pre-determined set of offerings turned a slice of rugbrød into its fancier cousin – *smørrebrød*, the infamous open-face sandwich of which my pronunciation was only marginally better than rugbrød.

Rugbrød served with pre-approved Danish topping combinations and eaten with a knife and fork is the most common lunch option you'll find in Denmark. It's almost a compulsory food and there are high expectations from the locals that, regardless of nationality, when living in Denmark, everyone will eat it. To bring anything else in your *madpakke* is often the first (and only) clue needed to identify yourself as being nothing like a Dane.

In the early days, when I was fresh off the boat, my outlandish bread behaviour had been tolerated. Bastardising the holy lunch grail of Denmark by making up my own toppings and creating sandwiches, which had no name in the 'Danish Book of Sandwiches' (which I presumed given the strict adherence to the sandwich-making rules, every Dane must have), was politely ignored. But I'd sensed a change lately.

"That's mayonnaise," The Dane informed me, as he layered his rugbrød with a spoonful of curried herrings. "Not remoulade." This was offered by way of a directive and referred to the illegitimately matched sauce I was about to squirt on my bread.

Looking at the identical, upside-down yellow squeezie containers in front of me I remained confused and felt a hint of indignance spreading across my face.

"Does it matter?" I asked.

"Well you can put whatever you want on it. But the remoulade goes with the fish," he stated, clarifying the role of the popular fish sauce, which was only pronounceable when drunk.

Even with over a year of Danish lunches behind me, *smørrebrød* expectations remained challenging. I'd tried conforming to the standard toppings and combinations when I first arrived, but a year later boredom and the temptation to watch others squirm with my unorthodox creations became too great. I'd enjoyed going rogue, ignoring the 'Danish Book of Sandwiches', and mixing toppings no sane Dane would consider. On particularly brave days, I'd introduced completely new toppings to our household. Wild combinations, that included ham and sliced tomato and resembled something more like the 'real sandwiches' I'd grown up with. The ones with a second slice of bread on top.

"I think I'll try it with mayonnaise today," I replied as I squirted a large swirl on top of the rye canvas in front of me. Landing with a flatulate splat on my bread, I wasn't convinced I'd made the right gastronomy choice but decided not to admit that to The Dane right now.

Squirming in his chair, The Dane reached for the make-do butter container that hid among the gang of trusty food toppings in the middle of the table. It was filled with whatever butter he'd spotted listed as *tilbud* (on special) in the deluge of supermarket brochures that were pushed through our letterbox every week. He scoured the flyers with more enthusiasm than an 80-year-old in a bingo hall, circling the best bargains every week, to see who had the cheapest whatever it was we needed. Looking at the shabby DIY butter container, I decided to add a designer butter dish to my Christmas wishlist for next year.

Sitting in her Tripp Trapp® highchair at the end of the table, BBB was determinedly shovelling potatoes into her mouth. She hadn't worked out they were supposed to go on top of her bread and eaten together yet. Both of us were learning.

"Can you help me with my taxes tonight?" I asked The Dane, hoping my ploy of distracting him from closer inspection of my plate wasn't as blatant as it felt.

"How come?" he asked, cutting in half a cold potato before placing it on his bread and decorating it with swirls of the flatulent mayonnaise. He then finished it with sprinkles of fried onion that I'd named 'crunchy things' because the pronunciation of the Danish name continued to evade me.

"I think SKAT charged me 50 percent tax for the freelancing work I did," I replied, wondering if it was actually a bit more than that. SKAT was the Danish tax department whose system I was still to understand. "What about the appointment with the Tax Advisor today? What did he say?" I asked as I placed a spoonful of squashed avocado, which a generation below mine would call smashed, with a slice of tomato on my next topless creation. It wasn't a sandwich to be found in the mythical 'Danish Book of Sandwiches'. I was having a rogue moment, gleefully disrupting the list of permitted toppings.

Enthusiastically, The Dane began replying in much more detail than my brain had capacity for, leaving me instantly regretting asking the question. My mind drifted as the white noise began floating over me.

Like Christmas nuts, preposterously difficult to crack unless you had a jackhammer in your pocket, the Danish labour market was continuing to frustrate me. I'd spent hours jumping through automated HR employment hoops crafting job applications that were never read by a human and at best resulted in an automated email. It was a crappy, inhumane recruitment process designed to make me want to poke my eyes out. As a newly arrived non-EU foreigner it felt like I'd been placed somewhere at the bottom of the employability list. *Or maybe they were just nervous about a foreigner disrupting the smørrebrød table in the office canteen?* Which was possibly a fair call. I was bound to feck something up and create an inappropriate rye combo. Although I had managed to pick up a few small jobs improving English marketing material for a couple of organisations. That was how I'd unwittingly contributed 50 something percent of my wages to the tax department. My reliance on The Dane to navigate the Danish bureaucracy to fix things was likely annoying him as much as me. These were all things 'New Zealand Keri' could have sorted unaided.

BBB let out a wail of boredom.

"Let's get you ready for bed," I said, wiping the now smashed potatoes from her hands as I lifted her up from the wooden highchair in one swoop. The previously transparent tray was now smeared with starch.

The Dane looked understandably annoyed I was no longer listening to him.

"Sorry. Tell me more once we get BBB in bed," I suggested, leaving him to clear the table.

Shoot. I forgot the mandatory post-meal homage.

"*Tak for mad*," I yelled back over my shoulder, hoping my salutation of thanks to the chef wasn't deemed too late to count.

"*Velbekomme*," came the 'I hope you enjoyed your food' echo from The Dane. His tone suggested it was within the socially acceptable window to acknowledge the chef.

Half an hour later, after convincing BBB she wanted to sleep, I backed out of her bedroom feeling like I was a bank robber dodging red security lasers, as I tried to avoid the squeaky floorboards. Making it to the doorway, I hovered for a moment checking if there were any signs of rioting about to burst forth from her bed.

Pausing, a fart (not mine) ricocheted across the room, quickly followed by a belch and then something I convinced myself was a snore. *Perfect*, I thought as I legged it back to The Dane before any other eruptions could occur.

"She's asleep?" The Dane asked with expectations much higher than mine.

"I think so," I replied while peering into the kettle for excessive limescale deposits. Deciding it wasn't yet at an unacceptable level to prohibit tea making, I popped it on. Reaching into the catering-sized bag of PG tips, I threw a tea bag into my Royal Copenhagen cup of perfect dimensions with its swirl of dark blue flowers. It moulded easily into my hand. There was something about this small ritual of making a bog-standard cup of tea that gave me peace. Even if I still needed night vision goggles to navigate teacup to table in the dim apartment lighting that the locals called 'cosy'.

Surveying the apartment, there was still plenty I wanted to change. My DNA yearned for curtains and carpet and doorways that didn't have a raised skirting board at the bottom over which I had to constantly remind myself to lift my feet. The belt loops on my jeans were also in a perpetual fight with the door and cupboard handles and hooked me like a rainbow trout every time I got close to them. At a glance, none of it looked that different to a home in New Zealand – aside from the ability to hear your neighbours having sex perhaps, something that I was beginning to accept was just a part of Copenhagen life. *But someone really needs to write a guide for navigating this stuff,* I told myself.

My line of thought was interrupted with the realisation that The Dane had been talking to me. He was staring at me expectantly, like a Cocker Spaniel waiting for its next reward, from the other end of the table.

"Well what do you think?" he asked as something caught in the back of his throat as he tried to finish his sentence.

"Huh?" I replied, deciding not to bother pretending I'd been listening.

"He said we should get married."

Well that escalated. "He what?" I replied as I willed my nose and eyebrows into a neutral arrangement. "The Tax Advisor gave you relationship advice?"

"Yeah, it'll save us some paperwork."

"Paperwork?" I questioned, unable to uncurl my nose, which had now firmly rooted itself north, in alignment with my tone. "Romantic," I stuttered. *Was I ready to save some paperwork? Would marriage mean I could rip up my integration contract if I became bonded on a piece a paper to a Dane forever after?* I furiously pondered the various scenarios, my mind whirling.

The only difference I could come up with between being married to The Dane and what we had now, was a certificate, a $20,000 bill for a wedding party and avoiding the need to call my 40-something partner my boyfriend.

Mentally, I began writing a list of pros and cons. A lifetime of being forced to accept nudity as normal jumped immediately to the top of the con list. Even if my birthday suit was what I'd come into the world wearing, my pearly white bum-cheeks were unlikely ever to warm to wobbling free in the land of Vikings.

Switching to the sunny-side-up list, I considered whether marriage would give me a jump-start on the living with a Dane thing? Passing the first few modules at Danish language school had me psychologically off to a good start in being Dane-ified, even if I still stood like a mute next to the Dane at the local café, forcing him to order our coffees. But with the Danish I had learned, it had made me feel a little closer to being a Dane – or at least someone who could live in a world of Danes. *But do they actually want me here? Do Danes like foreigners?* Plenty of my experiences over the last year had me second guessing if I was a welcome guest in the land of pastries and hygge. Even my achievement of producing a mini-Viking, a new member for their team, didn't seem to count for much. But maybe marriage would change all of that? Maybe I needed to put both feet in. Taking a breath, I reminded myself I had worked out a few things since arriving that shouldn't be underestimated. I had had some wins. Things like learning the importance of always checking my supermarket receipt (even when living in the Land of Trust). My hair had adjusted (or, as I suspected, given up) on the hard, Danish water and I'd accepted my new 'normal' of drying myself with towels that felt like cardboard. I'd accepted the long summer months, with the insane number of hours of sunlight, and willingly strapped the eye mask The Dane had given me to my face as if it was an oxygen mask. I'd begrudgingly accepted the anti-social single duvets, although would never admit I might've begun to enjoy the genius of not sharing my linen with my bedmate. I'd become comfortable being a monolingual in a multilingual world and was embracing new cultural bravery to fend off the daily *smør-rebrød* expectations. I'd also mastered the art of delicately replying to the question of whether I enjoyed living in Denmark, even if I still didn't know the answer to that.

"How much?" I replied, wanting to be sure I had all my cards in front of me before we completed any negotiations.

"How much is what?" the confused Dane replied.

"How much paperwork and tax will it save us?" I asked feeling like I was negotiating my own dowry. "And are you proposing to me?" I tried to get a hold on the situation. Our finances were recorded with great precision, together with our general life plans in a shared folder in the cloud I'd stopped trying to understand. My computer regularly beeped with updates while The Dane tinkered with it. Nowhere in that folder had I seen this as an upcoming agenda item.

"I guess so. If you want to put it like that. But it makes sense don't you think? If it simplifies our finances and paperwork," The Dane replied as he began tapping at his computer. "And if one of us dies it makes things a lot easier for BBB."

"Right," I said not knowing what else to say, while processing whether marriage would mean I'd have to learn a more conservative approach to eating pastries, if not just for the act of trying to fit into a dress without looking like a New Zealand mallowpuff. Could a pre-nuptial agreement stipulate that multigrain bread should forever be known as brown bread in our relationship, and that coffee with friends would never last longer than two hours?

"It's better for our taxes?" I asked, buying myself just a bit more time to find an appropriate answer.

"Uh huh."

I pondered. Then with all the efficiency one could expect of arriving at a Danish party and introducing themselves to the other guests, I gave my answer.

"Okay. Let's do it." I would marry The Dane. Sometime soon, to save some paperwork and hoped, with or without hygge, I'd find my place in Denmark.

Skat. As well as being a term of endearment for a loved one or to describe treasure, it is also the acronym for the Danish tax department, *Skatteforvaltningen*, otherwise known as SKAT.

Bonus insight: *Gift* in Danish can mean two things – married or poison. True story.

Epilogue

You probably want to know what happened next?

Nothing Like a Dane covered my first couple of years living with my family in Denmark and some of the more memorable and character-building moments that happened. As I finished writing this book, we celebrated our fifth anniversary of living in Denmark, so it's fair to say a bit has happened since the end of this story – although, spoiler alert, I'm still no closer to being Danish.

But I have begun to realise that while I am nothing like a Dane, I'm now also not nearly as 'Kiwi' as I once was. I've become a cycle ninja in the cycling lanes of Copenhagen, I eat slower and know that the fish dish always goes first. I don't talk as loud in public anymore and I wait on the side of the road for the green man to cross, even if it's 7am on a Sunday morning and the nearest car is 2km away (most times at least). I'm even blasé about seeing my middle name, Verena, splashed around here there and everywhere. It's a name only a handful of people in New Zealand ever knew. Those Danes and their ways have gotten to me, although not rugbrød or the dancing around the Christmas tree thing.

I can now almost comfortably navigate my way around a conversation in Danish, but I'm not fluent. It took The Dane over 10 years to learn English and to be comfortable using it, so I'm not going to beat myself up about that just yet. I'll just keep truckin along on my own language learning journey.

My pastry consumption has slowed but unfortunately it's not been reciprocated with a receding waistline.

I found a job working for the European Environment Agency in Copenhagen. Which, I agree, sounds awfully flash.

I still have an integration contract with the Danish Government although will soon apply for my Permanent Residency, something I can only do (among other obligations) after four years of full-time employment.

Then the pandemic happened. A crazy ride that none of us saw coming.

All of which moved me to a new mental state realising my fresh Kiwi ways have changed. The initial shock and survival years of learning to live in a new country in a two-culture relationship have passed and I'm now in the slightly rebellious teenage years.

I've realised I can still be 'me' and integration doesn't mean complete compliance to a new country's traditions. After all, you wouldn't throw a penguin in the giraffe enclosure at the zoo and expect it to feel at home on the first day, would you? It'd be lucky to even survive the first day. So, I'm at least doing better than the penguin. Each species has their own expectations and preferences, just like in a two-culture relationship. Which is why I had to start writing the next book in the series '*Nothing Like a Kiwi*'. If you want to know when it's out, then let's connect below.

Let's Connect

Writing is a bit like playing with Play-Doh: throwing a heap of words and thoughts on the table with the hope you can mould them into a piece of art – or at least something that's entertaining and does justice to the stories in your head.

But the other magic of books is that they live a life far longer than a social media post, or even ourselves. They are read, and if they are good, the thoughts and stories linger in the reader's heads for years to follow.

There are also those who only discover the book 10 years after it's been written. Perhaps they find the book sitting on someone else's bookshelf, in a second-hand bookshop or they stumble on an old article which sends them on a search for the book. Gina (my brilliant illustrator friend) once wished me well in the birthing of my book – it was the perfect analogy as I continued on the path of writing this memoir and enabled me to breathe knowing it wasn't meant to be easy, but the result would be worth it.

So wherever or however you have found this book, I hope you found a few good morsels of information that entertained you and caused you to nod your head in agreement or, even better, snort in amusement. I'd love to also know what they were – so whenever it is when you pick up this book, whether it's when it was first published, or in 20 years' time. If you enjoyed any part of it and thought to yourself, *I really should let Keri know*, please do. Write to me via my website or social media accounts below. I'd love to hear from you and know that moulding all that 'Play-Doh' (the words) and sharing my story was worth it.

And I'd be super grateful, now we have reached this point in our relationship, if you could take a few minutes to write an online book review, on whatever your preferred platform is. That one small act will help other like-minded souls find their way to this book and this very same page.

Epilogue

Web   keribloomfield.com
Instagram keri.bloomfield
Facebook   facebook.com/keribloomfieldwrites
Twitter   keribloomfield

Sign up for my newsletter at https://www.keribloomfield.
com/thechinwag

Bibliography

Surveys

Fewer bicycles stolen in 2019,
    Statistics Denmark
    https://www.dst.dk/da/Statistik/bagtal/2020/2020-
    03-09-rekord-faa-cykler-blev-meldt-stjaalet-i-2019

Facts about cycling in Denmark,
    Cycling Embassy of Denmark
    https://cyclingsolutions.info/embassy/
    danish-cycling-statistics/

The most popular names in Denmark,
    Statistics Denmark
    https://www.dst.dk/en/Statistik/emner/
    befolkning-og-valg/navne/navne-i-hele-befolkningen

Resources and Further Reading

Chapter 1 & 3
Websites and articles
The Cycling Embassy of Denmark
    www.cycling-embassy.dk
    The Cycling Embassy of Denmark (CED) is a comprehensive network of cycling professionals from private companies, local authorities and non-governmental organisations working together to promote cycling and communicate cycling solutions and know-how in Denmark. The CED was established in 2009.

Books
The Little Book of Hygge, Meik Wiking, HarperCollins, 2017

Chapter 5
Websites and articles
Danish Society for Nature Conservation, *(Danmarks Naturfredningsforening)*
    https://www.dn.dk/nyheder/6-typer-affald-der-oftest-ligger-og-flyder-i-danmark/
    Six most common types of rubbish in Denmark.

Chapter 8
Websites and articles

Denmark Canon *(Danmarkskanon)*
www.danmarkskanon.dk
A formative project that is to raise awareness about
the historical and cultural social values, traditions and
events that have particularly shaped society and people
in Denmark.

The Danish Whole Grain Partnership *(Fuldkornspartnerskabet)*
www.fuldkorn.dk
The aim of the Danish Whole Grain Partnership is to
create target-oriented and effective activities to ensure
Danes eat more whole grain and thereby improve
public health.

Chapter 10
Websites and articles

The High School Songbook *(Højskolesangbogen)*
www.hojskolesangbogen.dk
The High School Songbook was first published in
1894 as a show of community spirit between the
country's *højskole*. It has been continuously updated to
reflect society and the current times. Today Danes sing
from the 19th edition of the High School Songbook.

Acknowledgements

Thank you to everyone who knowingly or unknowingly supported me on this writing journey. You believed in me and my idea before I did. My gratitude especially to those who followed my writing in the early days and innocently asked me when I was going to write a book. I dismissed your question at the time because it seemed an impossible task to achieve. But I never forgot your question. It was tossed about in my head until one day, as I sat in a plane waiting to depart New Zealand, the words 'make it count' popped into my head. Your question was the push I needed to write *Nothing Like a Dane* and make my life in a faraway land count.

Thank you to Britta who told me I could write before I knew I could. Thank you to Jo and Josh, my editorial guidance from Summertime Publishing. Jo helped me nail the book title and encouraged me with her observation that my email humour was amusing, and that was what I needed to harness in my writing. Jo and Josh spent many hours editing and deciphering my sense of humour as well as my New Zealand English, for which I am extremely grateful. Both also admirably put up with my inability to ever follow our agreed style sheet.

To my wonderful global friends and family who followed my journey of writing this book both in real life and through my social media posts. You shouted encouragement when I needed it and gave me invaluable feedback along the way by sharing your stories and global perspective with me. *Mange tak* (many thanks).

A special mention to Erin, Gina and Catriona. All gifted writers, artists and creators who have provided unwavering support, enthusiasm, and wisdom as I wrote, edited, procrastinated and doubted myself. I am forever grateful our lives crossed in Copenhagen. Thank you to Lyndsay at The International for unwittingly making those connections happen and giving me my first writing opportunity in Denmark. In a wonderful chain of events, it was through these connections that Catriona introduced me to a fellow New Zealander who was soon to publish a wonderful book called 'Being a Distance Grandparent'. The author, Helen Ellis, quickly becoming a close writing companion and an invaluable sounding board as together we navigated our way in 'birthing' our books. Thank you, Helen, for encouraging and helping me towards the final goalposts.

Thank you to Julia and Liz for your friendship and helping me to navigate being a mother in Denmark. Thank you to Mark for the sharp edits and proof reading in the later stages and to my Mum for casting her eye over the finer details of the manuscript. If there are any errors, it is because of my final tweaks after they did their jobs.

A humble thanks to one of my favourite New Zealand authors, Danielle Hawkins, for answering an email from an unknown New Zealander on the other side of the world. Your encouragement and on point advice was greatly appreciated and will not be forgotten.

Acknowledgements

Thank you to The Dane for allowing me to absorb myself in this project for many nights as I wrestled my thoughts and words into this book. And to Eva, I hope one day in the future this book might explain to you (amongst other things) why your mother finds it impossible to say rugbrød. Perhaps one day I'll nail it. Fingers crossed. Love you to the moon and back.

Lastly my final vote of thanks goes to the people of Denmark. *Tusind tak* (a thousand thanks) for sharing your country with me.

Keri Bloomfield (2022)
www.keribloomfield.com

Glossary of Useful Words and Phrases

New Zealand Words and Phrases

Biffing   Throwing

Blimey   An exclamation of surprise

Bloke/s   A man/men

Boggle   Confuse

Bog-standard   Ordinary or basic

Chinwag   A friendly, informal conversation with somebody you know well

Crikey   An exclamation of surprise

Codswallop   When someone is talking rubbish, senseless talk

Feck, fark or frick   What one might say if trying to sound semi polite when they really want to say fuck

Garage Sale   The sale of used goods in someone's garage/carport/driveway

Ginger Crunch   A classic cake slice from New Zealand

Gumboots	Known in other parts of the world as rubber boots, mud boots, Wellington boots or simply 'wellies'
Hi-viz	Short for 'high visibility' and normally refers to safety clothes (the ones in bright fluorescent colours)
Having kittens	When someone gets worked up about something. It could be a mixture of excitement and/or of annoyance.
Jacksies	Bum (or bottom if you prefer)
Kiwi	A New Zealander (as well as being a bird)
Loo	Toilet (but you knew that)
Mallowpuff	An iconic New Zealand biscuit, light fluffy marshmallow sitting on top of a shortcake biscuit, covered in chocolate
Manchester	Items for the home made of cotton, linen etc. For example sheets, pillowcases, tablecloths
Nappy	Diaper
Natterings	To talk idly, chatter
Panadol	Paracetamol
Pram	Well, crikey who knows. It's a debate of global proportions but for the purposes of this book, I have chosen to refer to a pram as both a flatbed and sit up variety that moves anything from a baby to a toddler.
Puffer jacket	Generic term applied to any winter coat that appears 'puffed up'
Sequence	A board game

Sharing a 'yarn'	Sharing a casual story
Shenanigans	Silly or high-spirited behaviour
Smoko	A short break for a cup of tea or coffee
Sparrow's fart	Very early in the morning
Starkers	Stark naked/butt-naked
To call a spade a spade	Calling something as it is
Togs	Swimsuit
Turned to custard	When something goes wrong
Wop wops	Used to describe somewhere (a place or town) in the middle of nowhere

Danish Words and Phrases

Afkalker	Descaler
A-kasse	A type of insurance against unemployment
Appelsin	Orange (the fruit)
Apotek	Pharmacy
Barsel	Parental leave
Bodega	A bar or drinking establishment. The smoky and dark type.
Bolle	A bun/bread roll
Borgen	A popular Danish political drama television series as well as the nickname of the Danish parliament building

Brombær	Blackberries
Børnebolle	A white bun/bread roll. Can also be darker bread but typically children bribe best with the white version.
Børnehave	Kindergarten (childcare for 3-5 year-olds)
Danish Book of Sandwiches	A completely mythical book I created in my head as a way of explaining the very set toppings and order of toppings for making open rye bread sandwiches in Denmark
Dansk	Danish
Danmarkskanon	Denmark's Canon
Dannebrog	The name given to the Danish flag
Direktørsnegl	A type of pastry
Entré	A small entrance room designed to leave one's jackets, shoes, gloves etc.
Flyverdragt	An outdoor winter suit
Franske kartofler	Known as potato chips in New Zealand (or crisps if you're British)
Føtex	A Danish supermarket
Fjällräven	A Swedish outdoor clothing and equipment company
Gift	It can mean either married or poison (true story)
God nat	Goodnight
Godt Nytår	Happy New Year
Gratis	Free (as in free of charge)
Gummistøvler	Rain boots
Hej	Hello

Hej hej	Goodbye (yes, really)
Hej, jeg hedder	Hello, my name is
High wiz west	What The Dane calls a 'hi-viz' safety vest. Refer above to the New Zealand definition for hi-viz
Hjemmesko	Indoor shoes. What one puts on once they have removed their outdoor shoes (before coming indoors).
Hygge	It's a sense of comfort, togetherness and well-being. It is not just lighting candles and wearing socks in front of a fireplace.
Hyggeligt	The adjective of hygge (to be hyggeligt)
Højskolesang-bogen	The High School Songbook
Integrations-plan	Integration plan
Integration-skonsulent	Integration consultant
Integration-skontrakt	Integration contract
Jobcenter	Job Centre
Kæreste	Generic term for either boyfriend or girlfriend
Kammerjun-kere	A type of Danish sweet biscuit, typically eaten with koldskål,
Koldskål	Cold buttermilk soup
Lagkagehuset	A Danish bakery chain. Direct translation 'layer cake house'
Leverpostej	Liver pâté

Loppemarked	A market selling used items (a flea market)
Madkasse/ madkasser	Lunchbox/lunchboxes
Madpakke/ madpakker	Packed lunch/packed lunches
MF (midt for)	in the middle (used in apartment addresses)
Mødregrupper	Mothers groups
Netto	A Danish supermarket
Nisse/Nisser	A kind of pixie, gnome or elf. A Danish Christmas elf. Plural form is Nisser
Nordvest	A suburb of Copenhagen
Panodil	Known as Panadol in other parts of the world, it's a common pain relief pill.
Rains	A Danish rain clothing brand
Regnjakke	Rain jacket
Regnbukser	Rain trousers
Ris	Rice
Ristede løg	Fried onion pieces
SKAT Skatte- forvaltningen	Danish tax department
Skat	Treasure, honey/darling or tax(es)
Selvfølgelig	Of course, as in 'of course I love rugbrød'
Smørrebrød	Traditional Scandinavian open-faced sandwich
Statens Uddan- nelsesstøtte	State Educational Grant
Storskrald	Bulky rubbish
Tak for mad	Thank you for the food

Tilbud	Special/offer as in 'the supermarket has a special on ryebread'
Tusind tak	A thousand thanks
TH (til højre)	to the right
TV (til venstre)	to the left
Velbekomme	Bon appetite/enjoy your food
Vuggestue/ vuggestuer	Nursery/nurseries (childcare for 0-3 year-olds)
Værsgo	Here you go
90-års fødselsdagen	The 90th birthday

Other important terms

BBB	The name given to my daughter so as she doesn't complain to me in later years for using her real name. BBB is an abbreviation of 'Bilingual Backpack Baby' and was the name of a blog I established after moving to Denmark.
The Dane	My significant other

About the Author

Keri Bloomfield is a Kiwi mum in Denmark and a witty observer of cultural nuances.

Born in Upper Hutt, New Zealand, she now lives in Copenhagen with a Dane, their daughter and far too many bakeries.

She enjoys confusing others with New Zealand slang while wrestling with her lifetime commitment to speaking Danish.

Before Denmark (BD) she could be found enjoying a flat white under the guise of a coffee meeting in Wellington or Auckland. On weekends you would have likely found her riding her bike around the Miramar Peninsula or, together with her brother, organising a triathlon series in Wellington.

Nothing Like a Dane is her debut memoir.

You can connect with Keri through her website www.keribloomfield.com. Here, you can also discover where she hangs out in the social media world.

scan me